D0777519

When History Is Personal

When History Is Personal

Mimi Schwartz

University of Nebraska Press
Lincoln & London

© 2018 by Mimi Schwartz

Acknowledgments for the use of copyrighted
material appear on pages 223–25, which
constitute an extension of the copyright page.

All rights reserved
Manufactured in the United States of America

Library of Congress
Cataloging-in-Publication Data
Names: Schwartz, Mimi author.
Title: When history is personal / Mimi Schwartz.
Description: Lincoln:
University of Nebraska Press, 2018.
Identifiers: LCCN 2017043647
ISBN 9781496206305 (paperback: alk. paper)
ISBN 9781496207296 (epub)
ISBN 9781496207302 (mobi)
ISBN 9781496207319 (pdf)
Subjects: LCSH: Schwartz, Mimi. | English
teachers—United States—Biography. | Jewish
women—United States—Biography.
Classification: LCC PE64.S38 A3 2018 | DDC
818/.603 [B]—dc23 LC record available at
https://lccn.loc.gov/2017043647

Set in New Baskerville ITC Pro by Mikala R Kolander.
Designed by L. Auten.

To Carly, Kyle, Sara, Jason, and Karen
as history becomes theirs

Who lives? Who dies? Who tells their story?

—LIN-MANUEL MIRANDA

Contents

Illustrations

Preface

When I was eight or so, I dug a hole for a box of items I wanted the world to remember about being a kid on 110th Street in Forest Hills, Queens. Things like my Pink Lady trading card (a double), my second-favorite yo-yo, and a paper cup and string I used to telephone my friend whose bedroom was across the alley, opposite mine. Nothing I couldn't replace except for an almost perfectly round, white stone. I still thought I'd find a perfect one.

I buried the time capsule, in its sturdy blue cardboard, near the fence we shared with our neighbors, the Dichters, the only other German Jewish immigrant family in the neighborhood. I remember inserting a note with my facts of life, even though I knew about words blurring with dampness, ink smearing, pencil marks fading. I must have thought *Here I go anyway!* as I do now in this book, *When History Is Personal.* The objects, like the Pink Lady card, have transmuted into essays, but the impulse to preserve my small box of history remains the same.

"If we refuse to do the work of creating this personal version of the past, someone else will do it for us. That is a scary political fact," warns Patricia Hampl in her essay "Memory and Imagination." Hampl is referring not to the famous or infamous who tell the "official" story, but to those who shape history without making headlines. People like me, the daughter of refugees from Hitler, who grew up in Queens, New York, after World War II; went to college in Ann Arbor, Michigan; headed west to Pasadena, California, with a high school sweetheart named Stu; and settled on a small cul-de-sac in Princeton, New Jersey, where I raised a family, stayed married during the women's movement, found a career as a writer and teacher, dealt with breast cancer, played tennis, hiked near and far, lived with loss, and held forth every morning as a breakfast politico who rails from her kitchen table at extremists hogging the news.

I write to capture the world inside and outside my window, with an eye toward finding "the extraordinary in the ordinary," as Cynthia Ozick calls our daily surprises. Some are physically there, but unseen, such as the room-sized chamber below what I thought was our sturdy front lawn. Others are wisps of revelation, such as the kitchen heroics required for a Thanksgiving turkey, or the way one unassuming fact found on Google can overturn a favorite memory of first love.

In four sections, I write to bear witness to the history I've inherited, like family mantras, heard and overheard, about starting again in America ("Family Haunts"). And the history that surrounds me in neighborhoods I've lived in and passed through—from being a homeowner in New Jersey's first planned interracial community to eating dates in an Israeli-Arab village, listening as two seventy-year-old men—one Jewish, one Muslim—exchange versions of a shared land ("In and Out My Front Door"). And the history that springs out of conversation, told and retold online, on the page, or on a winter beach ("Storyscapes"). And in history yet to come as, growing older, I enter new territories of challenge, loss, adventure, and redefinition ("Crossing Borders").

The twenty-five essays in *When History Is Personal* are meant to talk to each other over time and place. Though the organization is loosely chronological, the power of the echoes and refrains matter more, informing and sometimes undermining a world I think I know. History, I keep finding out, has more than one version even when I am the only narrator!

Each essay focuses on a moment that matters to me with an eye to the history, culture, and politics that have shaped it. I look inward, as memoir does, to make sense of my world of family and friends, and I look outward to connect my story to the world I live in—be it on issues of assimilation, the women's movement, end-of-life concerns, racism, anti-Semitism, ethics in writing, digital and corporate challenges, or courtroom justice—but always as *I* experienced it, from where *I* stand today.

My inspiration for this approach comes from Sebastian Haffner's *Defying Hitler*, which I came across while researching my father's German village for my book, *Good Neighbors, Bad Times*. I'd read histories, novels, and diaries, trying to understand why democratic Germany was taken over by Hitler—and understood the usual explanations of rampant inflation and Germany's humiliation after the Treaty of Versailles. But something was missing until Haffner's account of growing up not Jewish in Berlin of the 1920s and 1930s put me there beside him: watching people he knew fill cartloads of cash for food, and become nuts on sports with its mania for winning and losing, and attend an annual masked ball where Hitler's Brown Shirt thugs terrorized everyone *before* Hitler was even elected. In these moments, filled with his personal observation and reflection, the rise of Hitler became real to me. I could imagine myself there.

Haffner, in his preface, argues for the need to personalize history. Otherwise, he says, we may fail to grasp how the political climate of everyday people can be quite different from official "weather" reports:

Official academic history has . . . nothing to tell us about the differences in intensity of historical occurrences. To learn about that you must read [auto] biographies not those of statesmen, but the all-too-rare one of unknown individuals. There you will see that one historical event passes over the private (real) lives of people like a cloud over a lake. Nothing stirs: there is only a fleeting shadow. Another event whips up the lake as in a thunderstorm. For a while it is scarcely recognizable. A third may, perhaps drain the lake completely.

It is through these private lives that we come to understand how the thunderstorm in one neighborhood can be a drizzle a few blocks away—and who sees a rainbow, who hears only the storm?

When History Is Personal is my weather report from the mid-twentieth century until now. It's not truth with a capital "T," as I assured my friend, a retired prosecutor, when I told her, over lunch, that I was writing an essay about being a juror in the Trenton courtroom where she had argued cases for many years:

"Show me what you wrote, and I'll tell you where you are wrong!"

"But I can't be wrong," I said. "I'm giving my perspective, remember—sitting in jury seat #13 for three days."

She did read the essay, told me what I didn't know, and I added several "Later I found out . . ." sentences. But I kept my initial version of truth intact, just as I did my truth about the twenty-four-hour nightmare in a New England hospital. What I learned later by talking to doctors and lawyers, I added, but without erasing what I didn't know then.

I count on my experiences clashing with what the world is saying. That's what creates the good tension I need as I write my life as nonfiction—forcing me to keep asking, as I did long ago with my time-capsule choices: How are my stories also the larger story? And where does my "I" fit in?

When History Is Personal

PART 1

Family Haunts

History never says goodbye;
history says, see you later.

—EDUARDO GALEANO

My Father Always Said

For years I heard the same line: "In Benheim, you didn't do such things!" It was repeated whenever the American world of his daughters took my father by surprise. Sometimes it came out softly, in amusement, as when I was a Pilgrim turkey in the P.S. 3 Thanksgiving play. But usually, it was a red-faced, high-blood-pressure shout—especially when my sister Ruth became "pinned" to Mel from Brooklyn or I wanted to go out with friends whose families he didn't know.

"But they're Jewish," I'd say, since much of our side of Forest Hills was. The eight lanes of Queens Boulevard divided the Jews, Irish, and Italians pushing out of Brooklyn, the Bronx, and Manhattan from the old guard WASPs of Forest Hills Gardens. No Jews or Catholics over there—except for a few blocks near the Forest Hills Tennis Stadium where, from fifth grade on, we kids all went to watch what is now the U.S. Tennis Open. It was our end-of-summer ritual before school began.

"You're not going," my father would announce before all such rituals.

"But everybody's going."

It was the wrong argument to make to a man who fled Hitler's Germany because of everybody. But I couldn't know that because he rarely talked about *that* Germany, only about his idyllic village where everybody (as opposed to the everybody I knew) did everything right. If my friends didn't have an aunt, grandmother, or great-grandfather originally from Benheim or vicinity, they were suspect.[1] They could be anybody, which is exactly why I liked them—not like the Weinberg kids whose Benheim mother was "a born Tannhauser," as if that were a plus.

"I don't care about everybody!" my father would shout (that was his second favorite line); but it was a losing battle for him. My sister Ruth smoked at fifteen, I wore lipstick at twelve, we hung out at Penn Drugs after Friday night basketball games with friends who were third-generation Brooklyn and Romania—and didn't give a hoot that "In Benheim, you didn't do such things!"

The irony of those words was inchoate—even to him, I realize now—until we went back to his village to visit the family graves. I was thirteen; it was eight years after World War II ended, and my father wanted to show me where his family had lived for generations, trading cattle. He wanted me, the first American-born in the family, to understand that "Forest Hills, Queens, is not the world" (his third favorite line). A hard task to tackle, but my father was tough, a survivor who had led his whole clan, like Moses, out of Nazi Germany and into Queens, New York. He was ready to take on an American teenager who said no to keeping a diary to remember. (I took photos and made captions instead.)

"So Mim-a-la, this is Benheim!" my father boomed as the forest opened upon a cluster of fifty or so red-peaked houses set into the hillside of a tiny, green valley. We had driven for hours through what looked like Hansel and Gretel country, filled with foreboding evergreens that leaned over the narrow, winding roads of the Schwarzwald. Even the name, *Schwarzwald*, which means Black Forest, gave me the

---

1   In this book, as in my previous writing, I've changed the name of the village, along with the names and identifying traits of people and institutions when it seemed appropriate. All else is true as I experienced it.

creeps, having been weaned on Nazi movies at the Midway Theater on 71st Avenue; but I was optimistic. Life did look prettier than in Queens.

We drove up a rutted main street and stopped before a crumbling stone house with cow dung in the yard. "This was *our* house!" my father announced, as I watched horse flies attacking the dung, not just in *our* yard but in every yard on Eelinger Weg. And there were chickens walking in front of our rented car. What a bust! My mother at least came from a place with sidewalks; we had driven by her old house in Stuttgart, sixty kilometers north, before coming here. My father, I decided, was a hick. All his stories of country hero adventures about herding cows with a book hidden in one pocket and his mother's raspberry *Linzertorte* in the other were discounted by two cows chewing away in stalls where I expected a car to be.

I can still see the stooped old man with thick jowls and a feathered leather cap coming out of the house with a big smile and a vigorous handshake for my dad who, looking squeezed in his pinstriped suit, nodded now and then and looked polite, but did not smile back.

Sind Sie nicht ein Loewengart, vielleicht Julius oder Artur? The man kept jabbering and my mother translated. He was Herr Schmidt, the blacksmith, and he recognized my father: "Aren't you a Loewengart, maybe Julius or Arthur?" The man bought the family house in 1935 from my Uncle Julius, the last of the Loewengarts to leave Benheim, and was reminiscing about how my father and his brothers, Sol and Julius, liked to play in his shop with all his tools. *Eine nette Familie, sehr nette* ("A fine family, very fine"), he kept saying.

I understood nothing because I learned no German at home. When my father reached Ellis Island, he announced that our family would not speak the language of those who drove us out of Germany. Which was fine with me. It was embarrassing enough in those days to have parents who, for all my coaching in "th," couldn't stop saying *Fader* and *Moder* in front of my American friends.

The man beckoned us towards Dad's old house, but my father shook his head, *Nein, Danke!* and backed us quickly away. I wanted to go in and see his old room, but my father did not. It would be forty years until I followed Frau Hummel, the blacksmith's daughter, up the narrow, dark stairs to a loft with two windows like cannon holes and searched the heavy, low beams for my father's initials—AL—carved in the worn, smooth wood. They weren't there.

"And here is *my* downtown! No Penn Drugstore for hanging out around here!" my father said cheerfully, as we drove past four buildings leaning together like town drunks. He pointed to where Grunwald had his kosher butcher shop and Zundorfer, his dry goods. "And here's the Gasthaus Kaiser! We Jews had wonderful Purim and Shavuot dances here with green branches and ferns and flowers like marbles in candlelight." I could picture Mr. Grunwald—he sold sausages in Queens—but I could not picture my big-bellied, bald-headed dad dancing, a kid like me.

We turned into an alley and stopped next to a gray building with stone columns, like sentinels, on each side of the doorway, and what looked like railroad ties set into stone corners. I wouldn't have noticed it among the houses.

"Here is where we spent every Shabbat." My dad got us out of the car to look at his old synagogue. He pointed to a Hebrew inscription carved into a stone plaque above the doorway: "How great is God's house and the doorway to Heaven," he translated haltingly in his rusty Hebrew. Right below was a wooden beam with another inscription, this one in German. It said the same thing, my father said, but it was new. He'd never seen it before.

I found out later that the German inscription had been added the year before we came. That's when the Jewish synagogue was converted into a Protestant Evangelical church to accommodate an influx of East Germans, who, fleeing the advancing Russian troops late in World War II, had resettled into the empty Jewish houses of this village of Catholics and Jews. Keeping the same words inscribed over the doorway was meant as a tribute of respect: that this building was still God's house. But the 270 Benheim Jews who had fled to America and Israel were never grateful. Their beautiful synagogue was no more; that's what counted.

"Well at least it didn't become a gymnasium or a horse stable like in other villages," one villager told me huffily in 1993 when I first returned to Benheim on my own. We were in the former mayor's living room. Two other villagers nodded vigorously, but a lively fourth woman, who said she had lived next door to my great-uncle, disagreed: "*Na Ja*, I wouldn't be so happy if our Catholic church became a mosque—and believe me, we have plenty of Turks here now . . ."

"They are our new Jews," the former mayor's wife interjected.

"*Na Ja*." The lively woman shrugged and continued, "I wouldn't feel good just because the Moslems said our church was still God's house!"

They pointed to "the Moslems" outside: four bearded men squatting around a table sipping Turkish coffee in a terraced yard below the synagogue. They had come in the 1960s as guest workers from Turkey and Afghanistan and by 1990, they made up 20 percent of the village. Quite a few lived in the old Gasthaus Kaiser, where my father used to dance at Purim festivals and where my Aunt Hilde and family had once lived above the restaurant. *This village, Dad, is more like Forest Hills than you thought!* and I wished he were around to discuss the ironies of migration. But he died in 1973 and didn't know that the "restricted" Forest Hills Gardens is now owned by wealthy Asians, and our house on 110th Street is owned by a family from Iran.

My father loosened his tie and wiped beads of sweat from his forehead with a checkered handkerchief. "And if you weren't in the synagogue by sundown on Friday, not a minute later, *and* there all day on Saturday, you were fined, a disgrace to your family. Three stars had to shine in the evening sky before anyone could go home."

I thought of his fury whenever I wanted to go bowling on Saturday at Foxy's, where all the boys hung out. Not that my father went to synagogue in Queens. The most religious he got, as far as I could see, was to play his record of Jan Peerce singing *Kol Nidre* on Yom Kippur, the Jewish day of repentance. And he fasted, which I tried once or twice but got hungry when my mother ate a bagel. She never fasted.

The sun was high, the car seat sticky on my thighs, so I sat in the shade of five tall, arched windows that someone had been fixing. My mother returned to our rented car, saying she didn't like standing in the open where everyone could see us. In fact, she would have skipped Germany altogether and stayed in Belgium with my sister Ruth, who had married Edgar, a Belgian Jew instead of Mel from Brooklyn. But my father had insisted on this pilgrimage.

"Aren't we going inside?" I asked when my father started to follow my mother. He was the leader on most everything, the man who, soon after Hitler was elected, convinced his brothers, sister, cousins, and parents-in-law, to leave Germany as quickly as possible; the man who figured out schemes for smuggling money taped to toilets on night trains to Switzerland—it took a few years—so that they'd have enough cash for America to let them in. Jews without a bank account of $10,000 or a wealthy sponsor could not get visas out of Hitler's Germany.

"No reason to go in. The building is just a shell. Everything was gutted by fire during *Kristallnacht.*"

"What's that?"

I imagined a Jewish festival with candles out of control. In 1953 there was no *Schindler's List,* no Holocaust Museum, so I had never heard about the Nazis systematically burning all the synagogues in Germany on the night called *Kristallnacht* or the pogrom of 1938. All I knew was that good Americans, in movies with Jimmy Stewart and Gregory Peck, fought mean-looking men in black uniforms who clicked their heels a lot and shouted *Heil Hitler*. And we won.

Kristallnacht, Dad had explained, was when the Jews finally realized they had to leave—and fast—even from Benheim where Jews said it wasn't so bad. "People felt safe until synagogue was torched, everything in flames." He became quiet. I urged him to continue, but he held back, tentative. Not at all like him.

"My cousin Fritz . . . Do you remember him?" I shook my head no as a story began. "He lived in that alley," he pointed, "and when he smelled the smoke, he raced over. He was part of the Fire Brigade, many Jews were, and began shouting, 'Why don't we do something? Get the hoses!' Men he knew all his life were standing around, silent. 'Against orders!' snapped a Nazi brown shirt, a stranger. 'Except if the Christian houses start to burn!' He pointed his rifle at Fritz. So everything inside was lost—a Torah, the Ark . . ."

I thought about the old blacksmith who lived in our house. Was he there? Was he one of those firemen? Why was he so friendly if he hated the Jews? "These people weren't from our village," my father said quickly. "They were thugs from outside, brought in trucks by the Nazis to do their dirty work."

My father, already in America by then, had this assurance from Benheim Jews who, like Fritz, had left as soon after *Kristallnacht* as they could get exit visas. "The Benheimers would not do such a thing!" said many who resettled in New York.

My father opened the car door. "In fact, many Christians helped the Jews fix the store and house windows also smashed that night. For that, they got in trouble. Everyone who helped was sent to the front as cannon fodder."

"What's that?" I asked.

"It's what you feed to guns, so they shoot."

I imagined a young man being stuffed into a cannon, like at the circus, and aimed at American guns, his mother in the red doorway of the house we just passed, getting a telegram, crying like in the movies. But I wasn't going to feel sorry, not when they let the synagogue burn.

Years later I would hear this term "cannon fodder" used again and again by Benheim Jews—and always with the same "broken window" story. It was as if they had decided collectively on this tale and how it illustrated that their non-Jewish neighbors meant well. "It wasn't their fault. They were afraid, too," they'd say with more sympathy than anger. But, like my parents, the Jews who returned to Benheim to visit the family graves did so quickly, never wanting to stand and talk out in the open or reenter old rooms of memory.

I was hungry, but my father stopped again, this time in front of a shabby building with three tiers of windows. This was his school, he said, and it looked like my old one, P.S. 3, but mine had a paved playground and better swings. This just had dirt.

"We Jews had the first floor and one teacher, Herr Spatz, who taught everybody everything. The Christians had the other two floors."

"How come?" I asked. I never heard of kids *not* being divided by age.

"That's how it was done!" he said. The Jews learned Torah, and the Christians didn't. They went to school on Saturdays, the Jews didn't. "To high school, everyone went together, walking six kilometers to Horb." Not everyone went; only the cleverest and those not essential to farm work.

"And did all the kids talk to each other and play games?" I thought of Tommy Molloy in the schoolyard saying I killed Christ, but then he asked me to play stickball on his team, and I said okay.

"Of course. We all got along. This village is not so big."

I didn't argue about that! The schoolyard was deserted and, looking for movement in a meadow on the far hill, I saw a giant white cross, ringed by forest that kept its distance, like dark green bodyguards. The cross was new, my father said. It wasn't there when he was a child or when he came home for an occasional Shabbat after moving to Frankfurt in 1921 to work and marry.

I picture him leaning over to nudge my mother, who had been quiet. "Remember how we had to park the car two kilometers away and walk to my father's house? No Jew dared to drive here on Shabbat! Am I right?"

"Absolutely. You'd be run out of town!" My mother laughed for the first time all day and turned to tell me how she, a big city girl from Stuttgart, first came to this village for her cousin Max's wedding. She wore a red lace dress. Very shocking! "Everyone was whispering, but your father came over and asked for every dance!" Her shoulders eased with nostalgia, wisps of black hair loosened from her chignon, and I leaned forward, close to her neck that always smelled of almond soap, to hear more about my parents having fun.

My father made a sharp left turn up a dirt road that zigzagged up a hill and stopped in front of a low, rundown farmhouse with half a roof. We needed a key for the Jewish cemetery, and it was hanging on the peg "where it has always been," my father said. This was the Brenner house. They were the gravediggers who, before Hitler, had been burying the Benheim Jews for generations. A quarter of a mile farther, a giant stone portal emerged from nowhere—the kind leading to castles—and the fat key opened the heavy gate that led us deep into woods.

I still remember the sunlight on that day, how it streamed on the gravestones, a thousand of them tipped but standing in an enchanted forest light. It was a place to whisper and walk on tiptoe. I remember the softness of the ground, a carpet of moss and leaves, and the stillness, as if the trees were holding their breath until we found everyone: my father's mother, Anna, born Tannhauser (1872–1915); and his father, Rubin (1866–1925); both marked by sleek, dark marble gravestones that looked new despite the underbrush. And Rubin's father, Raphael (1812–1889); and his father, Rubin Feit (1761–1812), their pale sandstone gravestones carved with elaborate vines and scrolls eroded by time.

I tried to imagine faces: a grandfather who enforced strict rules about work, manners, and Torah; a grandmother who, in the faded photo over my parents' bed, laughed with my father's twinkle, when life pleased him. She had died when my father was not much older than I was, of infection, not Hitler, my father said. So had his dad, who refused to go to the hospital that was two hours away.

But all I could picture were Opi and Omi, my mother's parents who lived three blocks away in Queens and "babysat" against my loudest objections that I was too old for that. Opi walked my dog so I didn't have to. Omi made delicious, heart-shaped butter cookies and told stories of how they escaped in a little boat from Denmark to Sweden to America, and then to the farm on Long Island, and then to the apartment near us.

"Do you want to put down stones?" my father asked, placing small ones on his father's grave, his lips moving as in prayer, and then on his mother's grave, and on the others. He had found the stones under the wet leaves, and my mother, wobbling in high heels, was searching for more, enough for both of us.

"What for?" I asked, not wanting to take what she was offering. I would find my own.

"It's how you pay tribute to the dead," my father said, looking strangely gaunt despite his bulk. "The dead souls need the weight of remembrance to rise up to God more easily . . . If we lived nearby, there'd be many stones here," he said softly to his father's grave.

In later years there would be more stones, as more Benheim Jews came to visit the graves of their ancestors, but eight years after the war, there were no others. I placed a smooth, speckled white stone with mica on Grandma Anna's grave and rougher gray ones on the men's. My father nodded. Some connection had been made, he knew, the one he had run from and returned to, the one I resisted even as I laid stones.

There were Loewengarts all over the place, mixed in with Pressburgers and Froehlichs and Tannhausers and Landauers, the same names again and again, for they all married each other or someone Jewish from a nearby village. My father said he had been daring to marry a woman from so far away—sixty kilometers! But when my mother found a gravestone that was her second cousin on her mother's side, I thought: not *so* daring!

We were next to a wire fence in the far end of the cemetery where the weeds were high. My mother had disappeared, so it was just my father and I among rows of tiny graves, no higher than my knee-caps, their writing almost rubbed off. We were among the children's graves, my father said, slipping on wet leaves, but catching himself as I reached for his hand. I wanted him standing, especially with my mother out of sight.

Above me, I heard the warble of a single bird and shivered. My father pointed out a headstone carved like a tree trunk but with its limbs cut off. It meant the person died young, in the prime of life, he said, and I thought of my sister Hannah who died soon after the family arrived in America, before I was born. I didn't know the details then—how their doctor, also a newly arrived German refugee, didn't know of the antibiotic recently available. I only knew the sweet face of a four-year-old with green eyes that was framed over my parents' bed, and that she was buried somewhere in New Jersey.

I was glad to move back among the larger stones, worn and substantial, like adults. I saw one dated: 1703. You could tell the older stones, my father said, because all the writing—what little was left—was in Hebrew. The newer gravestones were mostly in German because by 1900, Jews no longer had to pay extra taxes as Jews, so they started to feel very German, as if they really belonged.

"Did all the Benheim Jews come to New York?" I asked, thinking about how many came to our house in Queens and pinched my cheeks over the years.

Many, yes, he said, but some went to Palestine as a group. Others went to Chicago, Paris, even Buenos Aires. We were now before a headstone carved with a broken flower, its stem snapped in two. He touched it. "And some stayed," he said quietly. "There were many, especially old people like my Tante Rosa who thought no one would bother her. 'I'll be fine,' she kept saying. Later . . . we tried to send her money, but then . . ." His voice trailed off.

"Is she buried here?"

He shook his head. "She was deported." I asked no more, for I knew what deported meant, had seen photos of Auschwitz in *Life* magazine. I'd always been relieved that my dad was smart and got the whole family out in time—except for this Tante Rosa. I pictured a handful of old people getting into a wagon, but no one I knew.

The sun's rays had faded, the forest turned gray and dank, and we were near the cemetery entrance again, standing before a large monument in black stone, erected "to honor the victims of the persecution of the Jews—1933–1945." No individual names were listed, so I kept my image of a handful of old people as I walked over to a memorial that had a face: Joseph Zundorfer, his features carved in bronze above his name. He had been a Jewish fighter pilot in World War I with many medals. "Shot down!" my father said, placing a stone on the gravestone, and I pictured a hero like Gregory Peck.

Eighty-seven out of the 350 Jews born in the village, not a handful, were deported during 1941 and 1942.[2] They died in the concentration camps of Lublin, Riga, and Theresienstadt; but with no names

---

2 There were 126 Jews in all who were deported if you count those from elsewhere who were brought to the village and then deported.

engraved in stone and no faces to admire, they remained anonymous to me that day. What registered to an American teenager who lost no one she really knew was the sunlight on my family's graves, and how a thousand Jews related to me were buried, safe and secure for centuries in these high woods.

"In Benheim, we didn't do such things!" suddenly carried more weight, giving me a history and legitimacy that would have made me not mind as much, if my father continued to say that line. But he didn't. When we came home, he took up golf and played on weekends with American friends who never heard of Benheim. Their world of congeniality became ours, and I was to enter its promise. "Smile, smile! You are a lucky girl to be here!" is what I remember after that as my father's favorite line. His magical village of memory had disappeared among graves that were not there and weightless souls with no stones of remembrance.

The Coronation of Bobby

God gave us memory so we may
have roses in December.

—J. M. BARRIE

We all have different versions of ourselves, depending on the story.
There is one of me at camp, crying in the bunk bathroom all night
so my bunkmates wouldn't see me homesick. Another time I am a
bully, putting a frog in a sad girl's bed. And there is the brave me who
jumped off Split Rock Gorge four years straight until, at age twelve,
the cowardly me stared too long at the rocks twenty feet below and
backed away.

None of these girls is false. Each comes forth, intact, from a pocket
of memory—unless something, often small, shakes her authenticity
like a shift of tectonic plates. It happened to a friend of mine who
found old letters showing she was not the loveless high school misfit
she'd grown fond of recalling. And to another, who discovered in an
album of college photos that she'd been way too thin, not fat at all.
And to me, while writing about Bobby the beagle and my grandparents, Omi and Opi, who lived together on the perfect farm, where
I felt perfect too.

Everyone called it "The Farm," but it was actually an acre or two of meadow, an old Long Island farmhouse with a screen door I'd forget not to slam and a copse of woods big enough to hide in for a while. Plus the chicken coops by the stream where Omi went every morning and night to sing German lullabies to her American chickens. She and Opi raised chickens there for as long as I remember in those halcyon 1940s days when I was four, five, and six, and we visited them every weekend.

I think I already knew they once lived in a grand house on a hill in a city called Stuttgart, which made me think of *stutter* and *stuck*. And that my grandfather sold fine linens and lace in his store on a big plaza, until they left Germany one night by train for Holland and then came by boat to America in 1938, where everyone—my parents, two sisters, aunts, uncles, and cousins, forty in all—regrouped in Queens, New York, to start their lives again.

They were my mother's parents, but it was my father, so the story goes, who found the farm in Babylon on Long Island, a forty-minute drive from our house if we didn't get stuck in traffic on the Grand Central Parkway. Opi and Omi were "city people" well over fifty, so it seems crazy to me now that Dad would put them out there; he wasn't mean-spirited. But back then, desperate for new life plans, I imagine my father announcing with his usual pragmatism: *Others just like you escaped Hitler and became chicken farmers here, so why not?*

Evidently many hundreds of urban European Jews reinvented themselves as chicken farmers in the New York area, but I never met any until years later in Edith Milton's memoir, *The Tiger in the Attic*. There they were, in her Aunt Lisle's living room: doctors, lawyers, and musicians from Limburg, Germany, who raised chickens by day in Vineland, New Jersey, and gathered at night to play chamber music that filled the air with yearning, "and when the room at last overflowed with it, it floated out of the windows of the little white house . . . And the soul of a vanished world flowed out over Vineland and mixed with the scent of the honeysuckle."

Omi, who played the piano nightly, and Opi, with two violinist sisters, would have loved the Vineland group and happily joined its musical forays into a better past. But alone in Babylon, my grandparents relied on smaller dignities to remind them of who they once were: Opi's white shirt and bow tie, worn even on hot summer afternoons, and Omi's lullabies. *Guten Abend, gute Nacht, mit Rosen bedacht.* My father sometimes called my grandparents "schlemiels" because "they cried too easily"; I never saw that, only patience and graciousness, especially when Omi let me, *gently gently*, gather brown eggs for her big basket. We had the same hazel eyes, so when everyone said, especially if I cried, "You're just like Omi!" I didn't care. She was strong to me.

Best of all, Omi and Opi had Bobby with his black-and-white tail that wagged like mad whenever we arrived. Unlike the German shepherd next door who bit me, Bobby was a dog for the unafraid, for those who kept trust with the world and chose welcome over anger, optimism over loss and betrayal—and Hitler be damned. My grandparents' lack of bitterness in choosing Bobby's good nature was a gift I absorbed without understanding. All that concerned me back then was Bobby's name. Real Americans, I announced with authority as the first American-born in the family, would call him Spot. Or Sundae, because of his chocolate spots on vanilla fur. Or Silky, for the softest, long ears I ever put my cheek on.

Besides we already had a Bobby in the family: my cousin who never laughed. He didn't visit the farm because he was from my father's side of the family, those who grew up in a tiny Schwarzwald village with chickens in the street. They didn't sing to them but rather liked them in sour cream sauce.

At my house in Queens, a faux Dutch Colonial on 110th Street, cars crashed on the corner on 70th Road, and the wounded ended up in our living room. Twice. At my house, I played dead at night, so that robbers in black boots who might climb the stairs (the first bedroom door was mine) wouldn't take me away. At my house, my sister and cousins, all much older, kept bossing me around.

But none of that happened on the farm with Bobby. Opi and Omi sold eggs at the farm's gate with Bobby at their side—except when I came to visit. Then he and I would take off for grand adventures, his short legs a perfect match for mine as we ran all over the place.

We'd hide under the porch, his head on my lap as we listened to the thump of family above us. Heavy boots, the efficient tap of heels, skittish slippers; they didn't matter. I'd stroke Bobby's fur beneath the shaking floorboards, he'd lick my face now and then, and we'd head for the fields and for the cave in the woods. Not exactly a cave, more like a large rock beside a fallen tree, but it was fine for lying down on the pine needles, looking fearlessly for slivers of sky as the birds sang. Maybe I thought of a wolf or a witch lurking, but I don't think so. These woods were for chipmunks and squirrels, and Bobby and I could handle them.

One day we crossed the stream—so shallow my mother didn't worry—and headed for the chicken coops. Once inside, Bobby growled, something he never did, and gave me a shove that knocked me flat onto the dirt floor. Something black darted through the air from a high shelf and disappeared into darkness, and we were alone again as chickens flapped and clucked.

"It was a giant black snake!" I announced to everyone eating *Kuchen* and drinking coffee in the farmhouse kitchen. "I'd be dead if it wasn't for Bobby!" The men came with sticks and hoes, and, yes, something had been there. A chicken was dead and someone, sometime, did kill a black snake. I never saw it dead, but that was okay. Bobby was my hero, braver than Lassie and Rin Tin Tin combined.

That he loved me best was indisputable. Every time we headed home to Queens, Bobby's short legs would fly down the gravel road to reach me. I'd beg my parents to take him with us, but my mother would say "No!" She had enough to think about besides walking a dog. "I'll do it!" I swore, as every child does, an oath no parent (wisely) ever believes. But my mother held fast until on the way home one Sunday night, we were stuck, bumper-to-bumper, on the Grand Central Parkway, and there was Bobby in the rearview window. I can still see him running between the cars, panting hard. "Bobby is here!" I shouted. "Stop!"

"It's true!" I hear my sister Ruth saying, for once on my side. My father pulled onto the shoulder, my mother grumbled, and he insisted: "Geddle, we have to take him with us!" And then Bobby was in the backseat beside me, licking my face all the way to 110th Street. How he ran for miles on the parkway without getting hit, I don't know. Maybe we were closer to the farm than I remember; maybe we were still on the gravel road near the farm gate. I do know that Bobby slept beside my bed every night after that, and I never pretended to be dead for robbers again.

Bobby had to behave, my mother said, or he couldn't stay. So I took out books from the library on how to train a dog. Sit, stay, lie down, heel. He learned all of them—and what power I, the youngest of ten cousins, felt from being obeyed. He never did learn to fetch the newspaper, but sat patiently tied to the post in the schoolyard while I jumped rope and flipped trading cards for hours before we'd race the six blocks home.

Omi and Opi moved within a year or so to an apartment house on 71st Road, three blocks away. Was that why Bobby came to live with us? I wonder now. The farm, I remember hearing, was too much for them to handle after Opi got diabetes and Omi had thyroid surgery. I pleaded that I would mow and weed and clean the chicken coop; we all could. But the farm was sold, and my dad, not a man to linger on what once was, spent weekends making business plans with his brothers, and after that he took up golf.

From then on, Opi came to our house every morning and afternoon, wearing his blue suit and bow tie, to weave on a big loom on the third floor. He made fabrics full of fine silver threads like the ones he sold in Stuttgart, and Omi sewed them into slipcovers, runners, and pillows for every room of our house. I still have two in blues that don't seem to fade.

Before Opi climbed the stairs and after he came down, Opi walked Bobby. Theirs were long, unhurried walks (not like my two-minute affairs), taken with great respect and pleasure up and down the sidewalks of Forest Hills. Lucky for me because Bobby, like my grandparents, was slowing down—and I was speeding up. I still came over to their tiny apartment for Omi's *Teekuchen* with extra raisins for me, but I didn't stay as long. I had discovered Sultan, a "wild" black horse at Stanley's stables in Forest Park, ten bus stops away, and went to ride him every Monday and Friday, feeling adventurous and brave.

I still loved Bobby, of course, and one day I crowned him king, like King George of England. I wanted the coronation to have a chariot of white horses and Bobby wearing a gold crown above a cape of red velvet, but I settled for a red paper crown and a long, silky scarf tied to Bobby's ears, as we marched on 110th Street. He was right beside me, his tail wagging, and my friend Paula brought up the rear, all with honor and solemnity as strangers stopped to smile like loyal subjects. A favorite memory.

Strange. I don't remember Bobby dying, as if he were still out there somewhere. I remember a funeral in my backyard, but it was for something small, like a goldfish or a sparrow. I remember the day Opi collapsed after eating matzo balls. "Too many and too heavy!" everyone said. I remember the call from my sister Ruth about our father, dead within minutes from a failed heart. But Omi, like Bobby, just slipped away. She was ninety-nine and had been in a nursing home for ten years, a fact without a memory. Did Bobby get that infirm? Did he die after I went to college? There is no one left to ask.

I call a cousin, the only one left, besides me, who knew the farm in Babylon. She reminisces about "everyone always eating eggs—hard boiled, scrambled, fried, and egg cakes—because Omi and Opi had to use every egg with a cracked shell." She remembers Opi dropping a crate of eggs on the cellar steps and Omi baking cakes for two days to use them all up. And Omi refusing to eat chicken, ever. She remembers a black snake coiled in a giant yellow gourd on the front porch, scaring her to death. I want to say *The snake was in the chicken coop, remember? And I saw it, not you!* But she insists on her version of the snake story, and I stay quiet until she goes too far. She doesn't remember Bobby. She didn't even know Opi and Omi had a dog.

"That's because I got him and you didn't!" I counter, deep in shock.

"Probably," she agrees. "And you got more rides on the rubber tire swing."

"I forgot about that swing."

I always believed that good memories, like the farm and house on the hill in Stuttgart, were safe. You called them forth as needed—through lullabies, bow ties, and coronations—so you could live with optimism. But Bobby's good coronation is gone, vanquished by a small fact I discovered while writing this: King George V died and King George VI was crowned before I was born; and the only coronation in my childhood was of Queen Elizabeth in 1953, which made me thirteen, not nine or ten—and way too old for pretend coronations of a dog. *Impossible!* I first thought. *Maybe I heard about King George on the radio . . . Maybe I mixed up George's coronation and death . . . Maybe we studied it in school . . .*

No attempt at logic helped. In an instant, the same dog, the same outfit, the same cast of characters morphed from a scene of tribute to one of parody. I, the loyal nine-year-old, was suddenly a silly thirteen-year-old, half-dragging an old dog down the sidewalk. My friend

Paula was not solemn, but laughing—*Mim, you are really crazy!*—while strangers scowled, making us giggle more. I *knew* this coronation was what really happened; the only part of my memory that held up was Bobby, ever the good sport, trying to please with a wagging tail.

My grandparents' house on the hill is sturdier. There it is, always intact, in an old album on my third floor. I thumb through photos of Sunday garden parties, my mother and her sister in pigtails, her brother in a sailor suit; sometimes Omi is at the piano, and there are plays and costumes, all within a thick garden wall. True, the Nazis were gathering behind it, black-and-red flags waving, unseen. But those grand afternoons, unlike Bobby's coronation, were unshakable. They had to be in order to cross the ocean to a Long Island chicken farm, nourishing a life of reinvention with dignity.

I wish I could reinvent the coronation, so I could again be the American girl, full of tribute for Bobby and my grandparents. But all I can hope is that sometimes I did walk Bobby the way Opi always did every morning and evening—with loyalty and no betrayal, right to the end. And if not, then maybe I can be close behind, still catching up.

Love in a Handbag

My mother kept carrying it around her living room, a shiny, new black handbag the size of a suitcase. Her frail, freckled arm disappeared to the elbow every time she tried to find something inside—and she was always looking: for keys, the photo of her ten great-grandchildren, her Visa credit card, her Inderal pill so she wouldn't shake as much. Some days she could barely hold a fork, it was that bad. But on this day, with an apartment full of birthday celebrants—she was ninety-three—Mom seemed fine. I squeezed past Cousin George and his sons to give her a hello hug while my husband, Stu, put our coats in her bedroom. Our kids and grandkids were coming later after soccer games and ballet.

"Happy birthday, Mom!" I hugged and kissed her, told her she looked beautiful, and then out it came: "Where'd you get that hand-bag?" I feigned innocence. "It's more like a trunk."

My sister glared from across the coffee table. "Through Ruth," my mother said, smiling at both of us. "We got it wholesale last week." My sister loved to buy wholesale, especially with my mother's Visa card. She once bought me three black sweaters on a wholesale binge. None fit.

"Why not get a LeSportsac, Mom, like mine?" I held my handbag up. "Feel this. It's so much lighter."

"*Yours* isn't leather! Mother only buys leather!" Ruth snapped with her I'm-eight-years-older voice. She now flanked Mom's right side. "Dad would have had a fit if he saw your *cloth* handbag!" My father had been in the leather business, selling cowhides and calfskins for shoes and handbags, first in Germany, then in America. So nonleather was high treason to Ruth, even thirty years after his death.

"Dad would have a fit," I countered, "to see Mom carrying a hand-bag that weighs more than she does. And is showy to boot. Dad hated showy." *How is it that after five minutes with family, I sound like I'm six again?*

This was the most that Ruth and I had spoken all that year. We had done email when absolutely necessary, such as when Mom fell on the sidewalk on 58th Street and ended up at Lenox Hill Emergency Room with a bloody nose and broken glasses. Otherwise we avoided the same room, ever since the blowout over the kind of help Mom needed after falling twice at night. I wanted the woman who took care of my friend's mother until she died, a lovely person willing to sleep in: "Mom needs continuity, and the dining el could become a bedroom," I insisted. Mom, of course, wanted no one. And Ruth wanted a rotating staff so that "no one would sleep on the job." She won, and from then on commanded a round-the-clock battalion; so when Mom called me almost daily to complain of "the waste of money" and "not being able to take a bath in peace," I'd say, "Talk to Ruth."

The birthday brunch was also Ruth's idea: "Come Celebrate. Gerda is 93 years young! . . . R.S.V.P. to Ruthie," the invitation said. Ruth had made it on her computer, her thing lately, and sent it out, without consultation, to everyone Mom knew in New York City, still alive. It arrived by mail when I was at Mom's, just getting off the phone with Jubilee, a bistro two blocks away, where Mom had asked me to arrange a small family birthday dinner for ten.

"Mom, it's the same day," I fumed.

"I'll do both." She was smiling at the card with her photo on the cover.

"Fine—and our family will come for the dinner."

That really upset her. "What would my friends think if both my daughters weren't at my birthday brunch?" she pleaded. The dinner was moved forward a week.

In the center of Mom's dining table, Ruth put a big "Gerda is 93" balloon surrounded by the usual New York brunch: bagels, whitefish, lox, fruit salad, finger desserts, juice, and coffee; but no *Linzertorte*, Mom's specialty for all such occasions. Ruth said Mom wasn't up to it. I said I could have baked it. Ruth snapped, "Everything came from Tal Bagels. End of story!"

Stu ran interference with two glasses of Scotch: Dewar's for Mom; Johnny Walker for him.

"So early?" Mom said, delighted.

"Why not? Being ninety-three is special!" Stu said, clicking her glass.

These two had bonded over Scotch long ago. And on *Berches,* her special potato bread, which she had taught him to bake when her fingers could no longer knead the dough. Only he knew its secrets. "Here's to many birthday toasts at noon," Stu said, as Mom leaned on his shoulder, the peacemaker she counted on since Dad died and Mom moved back north "to be closer to family."

The apartment, a small one-bedroom with an almost-East-River view, looked dark, the sun hiding in the blank November sky. The heavy brown couches didn't help. I kept missing the floral print couches she and Dad had had in their Florida condo, and how, rain or shine, the light came in from the sea. But she left them there.

Magda, a childhood friend from Stuttgart, came over with big hugs. She lived two blocks away, a huge surprise they discovered at the hairdresser on First Avenue. Neither one knew the other was alive after

Hitler. "Oh what a fine handbag!" Magda said with her lilt. She was carrying a similar bag, but half the size. My sister beamed, and I retreated to the brownies. "But I don't know how you manage it! It must be so heavy!" Now I beamed and popped a brownie (which wasn't bad).

"Arthur made patent leather just like that," my mother said somberly. Everyone assumed her gravity, while I pictured Dad, feisty as ever, looking at Ruth's bag and thinking, "Ridiculous!" A year earlier, Mom would have agreed, but after her breast cancer and a lumpectomy, Ruth's certainty kept overwhelming her. Ruth would call five times a day, or more, if she deemed it necessary, telling Mom, "Do this! How about that?" I figured I needed ten phone calls to compete and opted out. *Choose your own damn handbag! The way you used to . . .*

Two weeks after the B-day celebrations, Mom and I were at lunch—at Jubilee, where else?—and she stood to go to the restroom. "Will you hold this for me?" She dropped her giant handbag into my lap. "It's like a trunk!"

I loved those words. *My* words. "Of course," I said. "You really *do* need something smaller."

"I know." She looked at my Sportsac, a quarter of the size. "I need something like that. Can you get me that size?"

"I'll go this afternoon," I said, determined to find the perfect handbag, one to liberate her so she could charge to the ladies' room without a second thought. She'd be reborn as her capable, vibrant self, baking *Linzertorte*, making museum-quality needlepoints for everyone's walls, and working in the hospital gift shop, her heels clicking along, *Come on, come on!* as they did all through my childhood of trying to keep up.

I found the perfect handbag at a closeout sale of an upscale leather store. Eighty percent off! Better than wholesale! It was small, soft, and lightweight, in black calfskin with clasps easy to open and close and great compartments. Within twenty minutes I was sitting on Mom's brown couch, helping her empty everything into it. I showed her how her house key could connect to a handy clip and how she could put her Visa card into a really convenient pocket. "Isn't that better?" I was triumphant. "And it looks great!" My mother said it is the best handbag she ever owned.

She was holding it close weeks later as we lunched again at Jubilee— and I felt like the good daughter at last. Working full time and two hours away, I couldn't do doctor trips or take Mom on bank forays the way Ruth did, living ten blocks away. But I did this: found something Mom really needed. I took her hand, smiling, as she leaned towards me in confidence, beginning our usual conversation of regret and optimism:

"If only my eyesight wasn't so bad . . ."

"I could get you Books on Tape!"

"If only I could remember what I heard . . ."

"I could show you how to rewind it again and again."

"If only you could come more often for lunch. Life is getting so lonely . . ."

"One visit a week is all I can manage." For once, I didn't bridle with insult. "I live too far away or I would," I said gently.

For once, Mom nodded and squeezed my hand. "I understand," she said, and we walked arm-in-arm, slowly, with no clicking heels, back to her apartment two blocks away.

The day was going well, a really good visit—not like last week's elevator disaster, when, if I hadn't caught an earlier train by accident, Ruth would have whisked Mom off to lunch and a movie before I arrived. I intercepted them as they were coming out of the elevator, and then "You moron!" and "You brat!" flew around the lobby as if Ruth and I were again seven and fifteen, fighting over who got to use the bathroom first. Those fights ended mostly with Ruth paying me a dime to tickle her back, but easy truces don't happen with the elevator buzzing (we were half in, half out) and Mom saying again and again, "Can't all three of us go for lunch?"

Ruth eventually stormed off, so I won that round. But what bothered me was why Mom never mentioned Ruth at lunch, as if nothing big had happened. Was her short-term memory so eroded? Was denial her survival technique? Or—and this was the question I can't shake—was Mom consciously or unconsciously setting us up? After all, if Ruth and I agreed on Mom's life, what power did she have? She wouldn't get five phone calls every day. Or more, on days when I tried to coax back the young, radiant Mom who was framed in blue satin on my dresser top. Even now, I pass it and think of how my neighbor's children were in total agreement about moving their mother to an assisted-living home. It was a nice one; I visited her there, but she was miserable every day until she died.

The phone rang as we walked through Mom's doorway after our lunch. "This afternoon?" my mother asked, holding the receiver to her ear as I unbuttoned her coat, a Black Watch plaid I had bought her, lightweight but warm. "A concert today?"

She said good-bye and rushed to her closet in the bedroom. "Be careful!" I warned, afraid she'd trip on the area rug. Ruth and I have both told her to get rid of it, the one thing we agreed on—and Mom ignored both of us. Even Stu couldn't convince her. "Don't worry! I have great bones!" she'd say with her old, confident laugh, the one I thought I could count on, always. So far she'd been right and lucky. Five falls, many bruises, but no breaks. After age seventy-five, one fall in ten will kill you, according to the Senior Newsletter I found on Mom's desk. She threw it out before I could mention it. At ninety-three, fear of "what ifs" was no longer her thing.

Mom took down Ruth's handbag and tried to open the clasp, her hands trembling. "What are you doing?" I asked.

"Ruth is coming in half an hour. I forgot we had concert tickets."

"Why didn't she put it on your calendar? We had agreed to put *all* dates on the calendar."

"Maybe she did. I can't read it so well anymore," Mom said, breathing hard. I doubted Ruth ever checked the calendar—she didn't do calendars, preferring explosions of spontaneity, for good or bad.

Mom was holding Ruth's bag; her hands on the gold clasp were shaking out of control. Will you help me! her eyes pleaded. I wanted to shout out *If you use Ruth's trunk, do it yourself!* But the sane adult me helped to make the wallet, glasses, pill case, and handkerchief disappear into Ruth's handbag before saying good-bye. I left her sitting on the edge of her chair, the shiny patent giant on her lap. "I love you, Mom," I said, kissing the top of her white, thinning hair. She seemed so small.

"I love you too. And, please, be careful going home."

She pressed my arm—*To stay? To go?*—and I was halfway through the front doorway when the phone rang again. I stopped to listen. It was Magda. My mother started saying how upset she was, how she was forgetting everything, and how exhausting it was keeping both her daughters happy. "If only they could get along!" And that's when I let the door slam behind me, giving into the child I was, muttering, "It's not my fault."

It was Ruth who cleared out Mom's closet after Mom died, taking our handbags to wherever. When I saw the neat rows of suits, blouses, dresses, and the handbags on the shelf, leaning on each other, I couldn't do it and let Ruth take over. "I'll do the photos," I said, and we didn't argue, as if that switch had been turned off.

Our lives were everywhere: framed on bookshelves, taped on her bedroom wall—Ruth had made large Xerox copies, easy to see when Mom's eyesight failed—and scattered in drawers, loose and in folders. One was labeled "Ruth and Mimi," and inside, there we were side by side: me in ringlets, she with her big smile. And on the driveway in Forest Hills: Ruth, a sexy fifteen in a peasant blouse with one shoulder bare, posing with a high school boyfriend, Barry, while I, at seven, hugged my dog, Bobby. And standing close together at her wedding, and then at mine. And on the beach in Florida with husbands and kids. Each image returned the moment except for one oversized photo, half-bent in a drawer: of Mom, Ruth and me on my living room couch in Princeton. Our shoulders are touching. Mom is in the middle, and we are smiling—not fake "Say Cheese" smiles, but ones full of easy camaraderie. *When was Ruth even there? It wasn't taken years ago!*

We three are now framed on a shelf above my TV. I did it after Ruth died five months after Mom, in California, on Thanksgiving, surprising us all. We knew she had emphysema, but everyone thought it was under control. Not so, her doctor told us. She never should have flown—and certainly not without oxygen, wheelchair, and an aide. But that was not Ruth. Wheelchair and oxygen tank in public? Not a chance.

I still don't remember the when or why of the photo, but I like the three of us smiling above me—and wait for memory to make it so.

When to Forget

I

Don't forget not to slam the screen door!

—MY MOTHER, EVERY DAY

True, no one wants to forget the teapot on the stove, the one that never whistles reliably as water boils to nothing. Or the oatmeal that crusts into permanency if you forget it's cooking while you take a bath. Or the names of things, like birds of the Galapagos you watched for hours ten years ago, especially the one that stands on one foot and sounds like breasts, Bobos something. Or whoever told you last week about a great new restaurant in SoHo—or was it at the South Street Seaport? If you remembered who told you, you could call.

Not that you are concerned (unless the house burns down). Look, your freshman advisee in the Yankees cap not only forgot to wear a jacket in the snow, he remembered his teacher last semester as "Mr. Something." You didn't try jogging his memory, sure that if he signed up for the course again, he would be fine. As you were fine when, in the middle of disk 3 of *Jude the Obscure,* you realized that you'd heard the same audiobook the year before. It didn't matter because you were hooked once again, eager to find out what would

33

happen to Jude and Sue Bridehead looking for love in Christown, or is it Christminster?

2

The palest ink is better than the best memory.

—CHINESE PROVERB

Macaroni and cheese. OJ. Shirts to the cleaners. Even as a newlywed of twenty-one, you made shopping lists and To Do lists, imposing structure on a scattered life. You usually misplaced the lists, but writing them got the muddle out of your head, most days.

As did the journals you kept in your thirties, until one summer night when you reread them. Whine, whine, whine about being misunderstood, undervalued, unrecognized—except on days that you thought yourself the luckiest, happiest person in the world. All went in the Dumpster along with whoever wrote them. Or so you thought until cleaning out a closet last week, you found three notebooks in an unmarked carton:

> Today I'm 45. Happy birthday to me. Do I feel my age? What does that mean? At 15, being 45 seemed the end of life. At 25, it was still pretty old. But today I feel young, with many options open, and the confidence to take them.

This woman is so upbeat—and you totally agree about this age business. As you told your friend yesterday on the tennis court—it was her big 70th birthday—"Don't forget you just beat me!" You said this while remembering the forty-two-year-old that you yourself had just beaten.

There were also entries about loving a trip to Egypt, and ones ranting about Tolstoy's "All happy families are alike." One stunned you:

> I'm afraid of cancer—creeping on my skin, under my skin, gathering into a silent mass in some dark corner of myself. But they say

you can avoid it by thinking positive, imagining everything lit up by lightbulbs, white blood cells blinding malignancies with their luster.

This entry was two years before the doctor found the lump. How did you know—and how did you forget knowing? You seem to have saved only slivers of self, forgetting others you could use, such as the high school junior with a pageboy cut and auburn hair in Stu's wallet. This younger you is kneeling on the grass on 110th Street in plaid Bermuda shorts, looking better than you thought. "It's when I fell in love with you," he said, when you found it. You are glad he still carries it around.

3

Memory, my dear Cecily, is the
diary we all carry about with us.

—OSCAR WILDE

You two were doing the Lindy at Stu's senior prom (he was a year ahead) when he landed hard on your foot. "Forget it!" you said easily, still feeling his whomp on your creamy silk heels. You took them off and danced in stocking feet, happy to kick high and swing fast—unafraid of more whomps as the lights kept spinning in red and blue. You don't remember the music or food—well, maybe the Old Spice that Stu borrowed from his father—but you still feel the cool of the dance floor and the fling of your shoes under the table for a night of freedom.

Much later your green Dodge skidded on ice across the divided road, spinning you into the phone pole, backward. The seat broke, absorbing the impact, and you walked away without a scratch. It should be your good fortune that overwhelms your memory; but no, it's the freedom of spinning that you can't forget, of not being in charge, letting thirty seconds last forever.

4

Forgive and Forget

It was on the wall in third grade: *Forgive and Forget,* in red, the boldest of three signs for how to behave. It worked well when Arlene Baker spilled apple juice on your homework and less well when Richard Pear took your pencil and stabbed you with it. You knew he liked you and wanted your attention, but your skin still turned blue. Then Arlene and Paula went for ice cream without you and said they were sorry, so it made sense to forgive and forget when you walked up to town as a threesome. But it also made sense to remember.

In your father's German village, there is a plaque mounted beside the door of the former synagogue, installed in the 1960s on what had become the Protestant Evangelical Church: *Zur Erinnerung und Mahnung* ("Remember and Be Forewarned") followed by: "We remember our fellow Jewish citizens who were victims of the Nazi terror regime and those who lost their home."

You are glad it is there, one of many efforts by the villagers not to forget the lessons of the Nazi past. Herr Stolle, the villager who showed you the plaque, was a young soldier in Hitler's army and quick to say he'd been "an aerial photographer in France, not on the Eastern Front." Since retirement, he'd been documenting the history of his former Jewish neighbors and gave you a packet of your family's past: handwritten insurance records, tax receipts from 1894, a family tree going back to 1750; photographs of the gravestones of grandparents and great-grandparents in the old Jewish cemetery in the woods.

You were moved by his efforts, a man who also arranged a visit into your grandfather's house, took you to the graves of your ancestors and then to his home, where his wife served the same *Linzertorte* your mother and aunts baked in Queens. You felt pleased but also guilty as you sat before a large picture window, looking out at the red rooftops of a village that deported one quarter of its Jews—and you struggled with how much to forgive and forget.

5

Nothing fixes a thing so intensely
in memory as the wish to forget it.

—MONTAIGNE

Forget the twinge below the rib when you twist. And the '*what ifs*' of a growth that seems bigger, until you finally go to the doctor, who does all the tests while you imagine your funeral—until you hear, "It is nothing. Forget about it!" And you do—until another twist, another twinge.

Forget the scar, now whitish with just a hint of angry red across your chest. Forget your old definitions of beauty, the ones you had wearing tight, angora sweaters to Foxy's bowling alley, your breasts bigger than Arlene Baker's. The pain of the knife, the raw wound wrapped under stiff gauze, that's gone, but the phantom left breast keeps returning in the night mirror, a soft, milky white.

Forget your mother's last year, and the fury you felt that you were no longer the good daughter because she was no longer the mother with the bright smile framed on your dresser, her hair thick and black. She'd been so reasonable and charming before her eyes and memory failed; before her hair became a dull, wispy gray; before she stopped listening to you; before the day when you had to go to Riverside Funeral Chapel to identify her in the coffin, face up, rigid, an unrelenting someone you didn't know, even as you nodded, "Yes, that's her."

"It's Just Like Benheim"

Do you know how my mother did the wash? She
had a big kettle. We took it into the yard, put
water in it, and lit a fire—and then the wash
got cooked. It took two days . . . so we didn't
change our clothes so often.

—SOPHIE MARX, FROM 179TH STREET

Sophie Marx, who grew up five houses from my father, was talking about their village of 1,200: "Not even toilet paper we had!" But more than primitivism, she remembered "the wonderful mountains and forests . . . and wild flowers dancing in the meadow" outside her window. And the intimacy of community: "Each knew each. The whole town, the Gentiles too. They were nice, very nice. Then Hitler came."

Sophie now lived in a dimly lit, two-bedroom apartment—"1B, first left after the front door"—a few blocks south of the George Washington Bridge. Her graffiti-covered, stone apartment house was, in 1991, in the heart of Washington Heights, where German-speaking Jews, fleeing Hitler, settled during the 1930s. The Germans who weren't Jewish settled in Yorktown, six miles south and east, and the German Jews who wanted to forget Germany forever, like my family, headed for Queens twelve miles away.

As I child, I shied away from the Sophies who visited with their heavy accents and too-big smiles; they scared me. Yet here I was, four decades later, asking Sophie (and whoever else was left) about her memories of village life before, during, and after Nazi times. It was the subject I'd always avoided—until I saw the village Torah in a glass case in Israel, open and legible despite a gash mark. It had been rescued on *Kristallnacht* "not by the Jews, but by their Christian neighbors." So said the old man showing me around; he'd known my father as a boy in Benheim. "After the war, they sent it to us here." We were in the Memorial Room of the moshav where two dozen Benheimers fled at the same time my parents came to America. I wished my father were alive to ask about the story, but all I had was his echo from 110th Street: "In Benheim, before Hitler, we all got along" followed by a new command: "Find out more!"

I was almost too late. When Sophie arrived in New York City in 1939, there were fifty Benheim Jews within twenty city blocks, offering each other solace and information about where to shop, register children for school, find a doctor, a job, a post office, an English class. Most had died or moved away, and Sophie, the last German Jew in her building, had neighbors from Puerto Rico and Mexico. "Very nice people," she assured me, an eighty-six-year-old who still ran her own household, "especially since Hella died. You remember Hella? Hella Loewengart? Your father's second cousin?" I looked blank. "No? She lived in 3B."

Like everyone from Benheim, Sophie was playing the genealogy game, assuming that, as *die Tochter (daughter) von Artur Loewengart,* I had mastered the lineage of all 350 Jews who once lived in Benheim. The upside was that Sophie—whom I first met the week before at a Benheim gathering, now down to twenty people—welcomed me like a favorite daughter.

I was struck by how upbeat she was. If I walked past Sophie outside, on the cement sidewalks dotted with overflowing garbage cans, I would have seen an old, thin, hunched woman in a baggy dress, taking painfully small steps from a once-broken pelvis (she had been mugged), and thought how miserable she must be. And yet she was "full of beans," as my grandmother Omi loved to say; it was her favorite compliment. Sophie was the first really old person I'd talked to lately. For years, I had whizzed by their slowness, barely looking back. No time. But lately I'd begun glancing over my shoulder more, as if there were something I had missed.

We were sitting next to a window that overlooked a phone booth and a spindly tree. This window was Sophie's favorite spot, she said, "Just like in Benheim." Always sick with asthma as a child, Sophie spent many hours gazing, while her friends played in meadows she could only look at. "I learned to make do with less," she said without bitterness.

"Do you think my car is safe there?" I asked. My eyes were on two teenagers rolling joints on the hood of my Honda.

"*Ach*, safe is no place." Sophie waved, and a hefty boy waved back. "*Aber Pablo ist ein* good boy. *Sehr gut.*" She realized she'd switched languages, grimaced and switched back. "Pablo is a good boy. His family lives upstairs. Spanish people, wonderful to me." She told how Pablo's father, the super, brought her the newspaper in the morning. And how another neighbor in 3E lent her a vacuum cleaner because hers had been broken for weeks. She brought him cookies. "We make do," she said, patting my hand, "just like in Benheim."

It is a big leap from Benheim to 179th Street, but the connection clearly cheered her. Stuck all day in a dark room—brown sofa, brown chair, brown rug, even the window light seemed swallowed up by brownness—Sophie spoke as if wild flowers still danced outside.

On the sideboard sat a framed photo of a younger Sophie, shapely and smiling, hair tightly permed, her head tipped towards a man with a moon face and wired glasses. "Your husband?" I asked. She nodded. Fritz was born in Strasbourg and had a French passport, so that's how they got out. "The German quota was full. We would have been trapped." Fritz came first (an uncle in Ohio sent enough for one fare) and borrowed from other Benheimers, $50 here, $20 there, until he could pay for Sophie's ticket. She worked every weekend for years to pay back the loan, in a small restaurant owned by one of Benheim's two former butchers. "I mostly washed dishes and made five dollars in two nights. Half I had to pay him, and half I kept. We were very poor, so poor we almost gave away our baby."

She spoke so softly I almost missed it. "Gave away your baby?" I couldn't hide my shock. My parents managed to smuggle money out of Germany to have a cushion; they never faced such desperation.

"*Ja,*" she said, embarrassed. "We were lucky." She brightened. "Self Help, the refugee organization, and the other Benheimers saved us!" Now she was all smiles, so quick was the shift from dark to light: "They paid for a tiny apartment with central heat, a gas stove, an electric refrigerator—all miracles after Benheim. We had no kitchen cabinets. Everything—vinegar, salt, onions, plates and cups, everything—all fit in the steamer trunk we brought from Germany! But 'we made do.'" This was clearly her mantra.

Sophie got up slowly and disappeared behind a screen that, judging from the clatter of plates, hid the kitchen. I watched Pablo clowning with a girl on the front stoop until Sophie returned with a small plate of cookies. "Strictly kosher!" she assured me. "I can't bake anymore, or you would have a *Linzertorte.*" She held up her gnarled fingers. "But I walked to the best bakery, the one on 169th Street." Ten blocks, I realized, must have taken her hours and felt honored, even though I'm not kosher. My family gave that up long before they gave up German, and so did everyone we knew in assimilating Queens.

Sophie watched me take a pink cookie. "It is good, yes?" I thought of my Aunt Kaethe, Aunt Thea, Aunt Martel (all dead now) hovering over me as I tasted their specialties, the world depending on my smile of pleasure. "Delicious!" I said, taking another, this time a turquoise with chocolate sprinkles that scattered on me as I beamed.

So far I avoided the Hitler years. A sociologist friend had warned me how good cheer in Holocaust survivors could turn dark and be hard to shake off. I didn't want to stir up painful memories, but I did want to know whether Benheim, under Hitler, was special:

"Did you have close Christian friends, growing up?"

"Not so many. But one, a nice girl, Inge."

"Did you play together a lot?"

"Not so much."

I couldn't seem to get beyond the one-phrase answers.

"Tell me about her family."

"*Ach,* her mother was a nice woman. She gave me Christmas tree cookies—and my mother never found out. What trouble I would have had!" She shook her head and smiled, pointing to the cookie platter.

I took another. "But why?"

"Not kosher, of course! It was a terrible thing, and I worried about it for months, waiting for God's punishment."

The power of kosher. No eating off plates that mix milk and meat, therefore no eating from Christian plates. Chatting in the streets, yes. Helping each other when sick, yes. But no shared dining "except for the men drinking beer at the *Gasthaus* owned by Jews." Kosher, I was thinking, helped everyone co-exist peacefully for generations by avoiding the intimacies that turn neighbors into relatives. Falling in love, intermarriage, they were the dread of both groups.

Later I learned how the Jews said Kaddish, the prayer for the dead, for those who crossed that line. And how the Catholics excommunicated a young boy who loved a Jewish girl and sent another off to a monastery in America. And how a Jewish girl, in my father's class, was kidnapped by her father and brothers and placed on a ship to America to separate her from her Catholic love. But "she jumped ship," the story goes, returned to him, and they ran off together to Chicago. No more than one or two outlaws per generation. I attribute that to kosher.

"So how did you and Inge become friends?"

"We learned sewing together in The Sisters' sewing class. They were nuns, and we called them the Sisters. Very nice. One was the nurse who often came to see me. The other one taught us sewing. A nice woman, very nice."

Sophie, who loved "nice," was clearly not a storyteller, but her sewing class affirmed "everyone getting along." Plus, she added, Jews belonged to the chorus, dancing classes, the shooting club, the Fire Brigade. One was even on the Village Council once.

I headed into Nazi times, hoping that friendship would triumph over politics. "Did you and Inge play together after Hitler came to power?"

"Not so much."

"But you still saw each other, right?" I sounded like a district attorney grilling an uncooperative witness. The same thing happened when I tried interviewing my mother—she kept changing topics—and my cousin Anna, who kept saying, "I was only ten. I don't remember a thing."

"No, not so much." Sophie leaned away, as if to get some air. "*Ich kann mich nicht mehr . . . Entschuldigung. Ach*, I'm sorry. I can't remember so good. And my English, not so good."

I changed my tack. "Your English is very good!" I said, hoping to up her confidence. "Did you learn it here?"

"*Ja, naturlich.* In Benheim there was no English. Only maybe if you went to Dorn to the high school. Your father, he went. No, maybe they only learned French. *Ach*, I don't remember."

Sophie's shoulders hunched. *She's exhausted. Let it go!* I told myself, but I couldn't stop wanting a Yes or No on the neighbors of Benheim. "It must have been hard to learn English here."

"It was. It was." She brightened at my sympathy. "I have now a home aide who comes two hours—she's Russian—and I saw how hard it was for her with English. Like for me."

Sophie moved towards a dark cabinet with a shoebox on top, ready for me. Out came a photo of her son in Staten Island, the one who went to college. Out came her house in Benheim with wooden trim and chickens in front, like my dad's house. Nothing new to take in—except that Sophie was now in charge of the interview. I looked at my watch, eager to go.

"Here is my daughter Elise." The photo showed a stern middle-aged woman with a cane. "And here is my grandson Richie." Out came a teenager with the same moon face as his grandfather, his arm around a smiling, dark-eyed beauty, hair piled in a thousand ringlets on her head. "They were married last year and live now in Mexico," said Sophie. "But next month they are coming with their baby. My fifth great-grandchild!" She held the fingers of one hand. "A little Mexican!" I listened for bitterness and heard none. The bigotry I expected from tradition-bound Benheimers wasn't there, overridden by love of family or by necessity—or just by "nice" neighbors who lent a vacuum cleaner and brought in a daily newspaper.

So that was the story, the one that slipped through the side window of my expectations. I didn't realize how planned questions could flop, and then, while putting on my coat or biting into a cookie, the story appeared. Not the one I had wished for about two little friends defying Hitler, but an odd American echo of that possibility: An Orthodox Jew, who walked hours to buy kosher cookies, made friends with her Hispanic neighbors "just like in Benheim" and ignored powerful religious taboos in order to be proud of her great-grandson, Miguel.

Grandson Richie, it turned out, came to live with Sophie after her daughter's divorce (another taboo in Benheim). He and Pablo became good friends, and when Pablo's cousin from Chiapas came to visit, she and Richie fell in love and now live in her tiny mountain village, miles from anywhere, according to Sophie's daughter who went to visit and came back distraught. "Never again!" Sophie's daughter announced to her mother. "It was so primitive, no electricity, no toilets!" Sophie sounded full of beans as she said: "I told my daughter, 'Don't get so excited. It's just like Benheim!'"

Sophie wasn't joking. This was how life made sense to her, a woman who "made do" for eighty-six years on two continents. And how, with her big smile, the one that once scared me, she kept fitting the incongruous pieces of Benheim, 179th Street, and Mexico together, as she passed me more pink and turquoise cookies. "So what is so bad?"

FIG. 1. My father's boyhood village southwest of Stuttgart, Germany, which now has a website in English about local Jewish history. In my writing, I have called it Benheim, but as the website features my book *Good Neighbors, Bad Times: Echoes of My Father's German Village* under "Publications," privacy is no longer an issue, so here is the link—http://www .ehemalige-synagoge-rexingen.de/en/activities/publications—and its real name: Rexingen. Courtesy of author.

FIG. 2. My father returning to his village in 1953 to show me "that Forest Hills, Queens, was not the world." Courtesy of author.

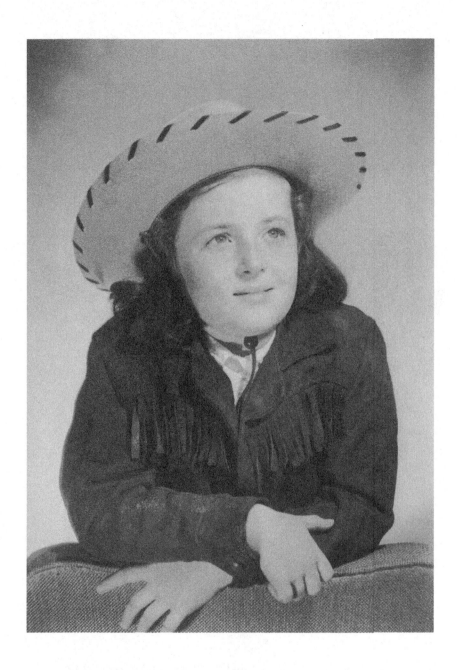

FIG. 3. My eight-year-old self, an American cowgirl "born four years after the family fled Hitler." Courtesy of author.

FIG. 4. The graves of the 350-year-old Jewish cemetery, "one thousand of them tipped but standing in an enchanted forest light." Courtesy of Synagogenverein Rexingen.

FIG. 5. My parents and sisters waiting in Switzerland for permission to enter the USA, 1936. Courtesy of author.

FIG. 6. (*opposite top*) Our house in post–World War II Forest Hills—it is "now owned by an Iranian family." Courtesy of author.

FIG. 7. (*opposite bottom*) Mimi and Bobby—Bobby was "my hero, braver than Lassie and Rin Tin Tin combined." Courtesy of author.

FIG. 8. (*above*) My grandparents' garden in pre-Nazi Stuttgart, "all safe within its thick garden wall." Courtesy of author.

FIG. 9. Omi, my grandmother, growing her vegetables. Courtesy of author.

FIG. 10. My mother and her great-grandson, one of eleven great-grandchildren. Courtesy of author.

FIG. 11. My sister Ruth, age eleven, and me, age three, in Forest Hills. Courtesy of author.

FIG. 12. My family in a garden in New Jersey, 1970. Courtesy of author.

FIG. 13. The bio lab of Forest Hills High, fifty-three years after I broke
Stu's pen: "He made me pay for it and asked me to the movies."
Courtesy of author.

PART 2

In and Out My Front Door

Every age has a keyhole to which its eye is pasted.

—MARY MCCARTHY

First Thanksgiving, 1962

Seventeen months into my marriage, Thanksgiving dinner was not in my repertoire. Not even memories of it. My mother must have made turkey every November, but all I could picture was *Sauerbraten* and *Kartoffelsalat*, not a slow-roasting bird in the oven.

I remember eating sweet potatoes with marshmallows; they were served to me at my best friend's house across the street, as leftovers. Delicious. Which is why I included this dish on my menu, using a recipe from Debbie, who lived next door in graduate housing at the University of Michigan. After a honeymoon year in California, Stu had decided to get a doctorate in engineering, and we moved to Ann Arbor.

Debbie also gave me her family secret for "homemade" cranberry sauce from a can. She grew up in Iowa, cooking everything for three younger sisters, while I, in Queens, knew only how to dry dishes and help my mother make *Laugenbrezels* out of big wads of dough we rolled, curled and baked into golden-brown pretzels. That was fun, but everything else in the kitchen seemed demeaning for the American cowgirl I had decided to be. Courage, to me, was charging with the boys through vacant lots like the Lone Ranger, not cooking at home like my mother, "the *Hausfrau*," untested by epic danger.

Or so I thought until the day Stu invited his professor and his wife over for Thanksgiving dinner. We had driven from Pasadena three months before and decided against the thirteen-hour drive to New York to eat turkey with our parents. So when Stu's professor mentioned that he and his wife were eating alone, Stu invited them over.

"You did what?"

"I felt sorry for them."

"And what about for me?" I'd spent our newlywed year commuting seventy miles to UCLA for a master's degree in literature, so my driving, not my cooking, had improved. I'd mastered scrambled eggs and hamburgers, but my only "company" dish was veal Parmesan— and take-out pizza from down the street.

"Don't worry. They are bringing the pumpkin pie," Stu soothed, as I dumped the unpacked wedding boxes on the floor, looking for cookbooks.

By 2 p.m. on Thanksgiving Day, I felt more upbeat. With tips from the butcher (rub butter inside and out) and twenty consults with my mother and Debbie next door, I had the stuffed turkey roasting in the oven and had made my mother-in-law's Jell-O Nut Mold recipe, which was thickening in the refrigerator next to a cranberry-orange sauce. For once I'd been organized and made it the day before, right after stuffing the turkey. I was folding mini marshmallows into sweet potatoes, humming along with Ella Fitzgerald or someone equally reassuring on the radio, when a news flash interrupted. Several bad lots of canned cranberries were proving deadly, the announcer warned, and people—did he say in Texas?—had been hospitalized. Everyone was to check the serial numbers on the cans.

My cranberry cans were in the middle of the Dumpster out back; I'd never find them. I had read something about the Pilgrims poisoning the Wampanoag chiefs on that first Thanksgiving and thought why take a chance? I'd go to Kroger market and buy two safe cans of cranberries. And if the store was closed, I would manage with the Jell-O mold, as two red dishes were not really needed.

I felt morally good, even noble, as I set the dinette table, concerned only that the paper turkey centerpiece I'd bought was too large. The real turkey was browning nicely, so I went next door to warn Debbie about the cranberries. I could have told her through the paper-thin wall dividing our dinette tables (this Quonset-hut housing was left over from World War II), but I was ready for a coffee break. All I had left to do was to watch the turkey, remake the cranberry sauce and open Del Monte green beans. No one had warned against those cans.

"Are you set?" Debbie asked. She had finished her chestnut soufflé and was chopping orange peel to add to the cranberries. That was her "secret" ingredient.

"I am . . . was—until I heard the news broadcast. Did you know that people are being poisoned by canned cranberries?"

"You're fine. Don't sweat it." Debbie had already called Kroger and its cans came from a different lot. Customer service told her the bad numbers, and Debbie checked them against her cans.

"I can't check mine because I threw them out yesterday when I made the sauce, adding your orange peel."

"Not to worry." She started to pour us coffee. "It's people stuffing their turkey early, sometimes two or three days before they roast it, that's the real killer."

"What? Why?"

"Raw eggs and bread sitting together inside a turkey is a no-no. *That* can really cause botulism. And salmonella. Bad stuff." She pushed the cookie jar toward me: "My aunt had a neighbor who prestuffed a turkey and all her . . ." *My sweet, stuffed fifteen-pound turkey was deadly?* I stood up and backed toward the door. At least I'd admitted only to one-day-old cranberry sauce, nothing more. "I forgot. I have to baste my turkey! Happy Thanksgiving!" I said, and was out of there.

An Iowa folktale, I told myself, dialing my mother to affirm this. I hung up on the first ring and dialed Stu in his campus office. He could pick up cranberry cans on his way home. *Should he pick up pizzas too?*

I hung up again after picturing my turkey in the garbage Dumpster. I couldn't do it; it looked so perfect.

I removed the paper turkey centerpiece and put the Jell-O mold in its place. It looked amazing, having stayed together when I flipped it. My mother-in-law warned me that hers once slipped into the sink and halfway down the drain before she salvaged enough to serve in individual bowls. Mine had made a perfect landing, right next to the cranberry sauce that looked luscious. Kroger had closed early, so I decided Debbie was right about the safety of my cranberry cans.

Stu was carving the turkey while I brought out the sweet potato casserole, still bubbling. "Oh, it looks delicious! Everything smells wonderful!" said the professor's wife, a plump, robust woman with glasses that kept sliding on her nose. The professor, a well-known scientist (whom I still couldn't believe Stu had enough nerve to invite) agreed with enthusiasm.

Botulism happens only after two or three days inside the raw turkey, Debbie had said. My stuffing had been in there less than one day. *It must be fine!* I had told myself after opening the oven door to a turkey, crisp, golden brown, and shiny. *It must be fine!* I whispered again as I scooped the savory stuffing onto every plate. I watched Stu swallow the first bite of drumstick, his favorite. I watched the professor drown his breast meat in cranberry sauce. And when the professor's wife ate the stuffing and asked for the recipe, my prayers turned to fatalism. *Whatever will be, we will live or die together!* I lifted my fork, ready to stab and swallow the white meat on my plate. But the fork, suspended in midair, headed for the green beans. I tried again, this time taking aim on the stuffing; my fork speared the sweet potatoes. Everyone's plate was emptying, but I could eat no more, even as I pictured myself as a widow in jail.

All night I watched Stu to be sure he was breathing, and the next morning I called the professor's wife, my excuse being to give her the stuffing recipe. She answered the phone full of thanks, so all was well, except for any vestige I had of heroic self-assessment. Not only was I a culinary wimp, unfit for the dangers of turkey and cranberry sauce, but I threw out all Thanksgiving "evidence" as Stu slept, rehearsing my alibi that the refrigerator door had been left open by mistake and everything spoiled.

I was saved from alibis because Stu opened his eyes. I jumped into bed, full of hugs and confessions about how I nearly poisoned him, and that's when I encountered true courage: "What's for breakfast?" he asked, and we ate my scrambled eggs with optimism, our marriage vows, "Till death do us part," full of new meaning.

Off the King's Highway

Off the King's Highway, now called Nassau Street, you'll find a cul-de-sac of six houses—and we're #4, second house on the left. It's the white Colonial, circa 1902, with black shutters, a large front porch with pillars, eight wooden steps that ice over every winter, and a cherry red door that was black in 1970 when we moved onto Evelyn Place.

There's a button in our hall next to the kitchen that rings on the third floor, calling the servants. I press it now and then, hoping someone from the past will appear, but so far we've received only written messages: "Helen was here, 1922," scrawled beneath three layers of wallpaper we stripped off the dining room wall. And "How's the old Princeton house? I lived in it from 1944–58," handwritten across the top of a charity solicitation letter from Chicago a few years back.

No servant has descended the steep back stairs our children discovered while Stu and I were in the basement inspecting the furnace with Mr. Mackle, the last owner. In dreams, those stairs lead to hidden, velvet chambers; in real life, they end at the little bathroom on the second floor.

From the dining room window, you can see what was Evelyn College, now a two-family house. It spans the cul-de-sac like an old queen with outstretched arms, and looked very tired for years—until Jeremy and Debra bought her right side. They found a photo of the original trim in red and green and wanted authenticity (he's a historian), but settled for deep green and gray, with touches of reddish brown—and convinced Paul, the owner of the left side, to follow suit.

It looks good, luckily, because the oak tree that shielded the front view died after the town laid new water pipes under its roots. By the following spring, half the branches didn't bloom, and the tree commissioner—who had assured the neighborhood "the oak would be fine"—cut it down and planted two spindly birches I can't get used to.

At the Quarry's Edge

Evelyn College, founded in 1887, was the first school of higher education for women in New Jersey and *Harper's Bazar* [sic] predicted "our country shall come to speak with equal pride of the sons and of the daughters of Princeton." It was to be Princeton University's sister school, what Radcliffe was to Harvard—except Evelyn College folded ten years later because of "moral turpitude." Or so the story goes, the one about its girls meeting Princeton University boys in the old quarry behind the college.

Natasha, who lived for fifty years on the college's right side (where Jeremy and Debra now live), had a photograph of the last Evelyn College class: a dozen or so young women in Victorian bonnets, corsets, and dresses with scores of buttons. There was so much to undo and take off! I can't imagine the logistics of making love on the rocky ledge before a steep drop. Whatever the "moral turpitude"—Stolen kisses? A few beers?—I've told this story first for years, preferring its rhythms of turpitude and scandal to the other story of the college going bankrupt after a diphtheria (or some say influenza) outbreak.

Recently I discovered a third story at the Historical Society of Princeton that I find most convincing. Miss Elizabeth D. McIvaine, quoted as the head of Evelyn College, blames "the opposition of Princeton University to any work for the higher education of women." Her father was the Princeton professor who enlisted his fellow professors to teach the Evelyn girls courses in classics, astronomy, ethics, psychology, and metaphysics—the same courses, with the same rigor, as they taught the Princeton boys. The girls did well, evidently too well. The boys complained. *You don't really teach them the same things, do you?* Trustees complained. Princeton University withdrew its support. Diphtheria struck. People whispered of drinking, boisterous songs from the quarry, and trysts in the hotel on Linden Lane, one street over:

Eva, Eva, l-y-n
Eva, Eva, let me in!

So it seems that all the Evelyn College stories are true when you piece together the shards of fact scattered here and there.

Princeton University, three blocks up the street, admitted undergraduate women in 1969, one year before we bought our house. My husband, who had just gotten tenure in Princeton's Engineering School, had no women taking his courses. Twenty years later, there were a half dozen or so; but by 2006, when Stu retired, half of his courses and five of his last six PhDs were women. He liked that, an MIT boy, Class of '61, who regretted the dearth of women beside him in wind tunnel labs. He especially liked, as did I, that Princeton's first woman president, Shirley Tilghman, spoke at his retirement party.

So thank you very much, Evelyn, whoever you were. And thank you, Miss Elizabeth D. McIvaine, who continues for me (despite a new story I just heard) as president of Evelyn College—and as builder of our house with its back stairs of dreams.

The Value of Old Bricks

Our street is listed on the National Register of Historic Places. Which means if our front porch keeps sinking, we have to replace four pillars and a railing with 110 spindles, so they look exactly as before. Approximations won't do, says the carpenter who came to fix what we thought was a wobbly front step. We assure him we value historic details; it's why we fell in love with this house and street that credential us, the children of immigrants, to enter America's past. But when this cheerful old-timer says, "A new porch could cost as much as a kitchen," we quickly agree with his suggestion to reinforce the old brick cornerstones with new bricks that are hidden from the street (and the National Register rules).

The old bricks might have been made, possibly, in Horner's Pottery, a once-thriving factory in this neighborhood that predates the American Revolution. Pots, pie plates, jugs, and bricks came from the quarry clay and gave our historic district its name: Jugtown. It's hard to imagine our quiet, little street as the center of a town with two quarries, a clay pit, the Horner factory, a tavern, hotel, carriage shop, tannery, grocery store, firehouse, hay press, smithy, bakery, chapel, two schools, and two doctors. How does that happen? One world morphs into another with barely a sign, save for the pale green plaques mounted on the eighteenth-century house fronts scattered around the neighborhood.

I did unearth two pottery shards while I was planting hosta near our garage. The shards sit on the shelf of our screened porch between a dozen rocks, mostly obsidian and garnet, which we "mined" in Maine on a rainy vacation with two small, restless children. There are also two arrowheads from a summer trip out West. And fossilized seashells found during our sabbatical year in Israel, 1972. And what we think is an ancient Greek glass perfume bottle, the size of a thumb, that our daughter Julie found sticking out of a seawall near the port of Acco when she was nine. Same trip. It has kept its luminous, silvery green even with its glued cracks after one of us dropped it.

They are all mixed up, these rocks and relics: half dreams, half history; untested and undated. Vessels of memory we relish chipped, cracked, or whole.

Blue Wallpaper

The wallpaper came with the house: blue and white vines on our bedroom walls. Not my style. I am more a white-wall girl, or else give me subtle halftones, more texture than pattern. Yet here was a kind of modern Colonial print that looked new even though the Mackles put it up five years before we came.

Someday we'll change it, we said then, but it never happened. Decades later we see it every morning as the sun slants its way through the window shades. And every night the shadows of the dogwood tree sway across cheerful shapes that darken when we turn off the reading lights.

The wallpaper looks new, that's why. Not a crack of plaster shows through, not even a hint—and we've done no more than repaint the ceiling and window trim every five or seven years. Who would mess with that, even if the style is not yours? You make it work, and after a while you can't imagine sleeping in a room of white walls.

Above the Mantelpiece

One wall in the bedroom, over the fireplace, is painted a solid blue. And Karma is framed there, our purebred collie, who arrived one day out of nowhere. On my twenty-seventh birthday! She is nose-to-nose with our son, Alan, when he was five or so. And there's Dad with his handkerchief tied as a hat, rowing me across the lake on the day I passed my swim test at Camp Inawood. And Stu and his kid brother, Howie, wearing cowboy hats, as they share a shaggy pony in Brooklyn, while mother Rose stands close, a stacked, sexy blonde of the 1940s. And my grandparents, Opi and Omi, sitting up straight as always, smiling with Old World propriety at a family dinner. And my mother, looking confident and younger than I do now. And our daughter Julie wearing her Northwestern University graduation cap, a tassel dangling forward, her proud Dad's arm around her. And Charlie, Stu's father, bare-chested, at Coney Island, a young hunk of a guy in the 1920s. And my sister Ruth and I standing in front of the flowered chuppah when I, at ten, was maid of honor at her wedding. And Ruth and Hannah, the sister I never knew, who died of strep throat the year my family came to America. Here they are playing on a Swiss ski slope, a pair of dark-haired, little girls in matching sweaters that my mother knit, their tiny, fur collars black against the snow. I see them all from my pillow, morning and night: those who are gone are not gone, and what once happened is still happening.

Carved Beams, Hidden Tunnels

"George Washington," Alan announced at age seven, "slept at Hugh's house." Hugh, age nine, lived around the corner and evidently showed Alan "GW," carved into a low beam in Hugh's basement. I never saw it, but I did see a photo of "1730" carved into the wooden mantelpiece in Hugh's living room. The house was built in the 1700s, and the photograph was in a local history book along with a mention of Washington quartering his soldiers in our neighborhood. So Alan's GW story, like the two wooden beam stories, and the three Evelyn College stories, all feel alive around me.

As does the story of the Underground Railroad, which was once across the street from Hugh's house. Secret rooms hid runaway slaves heading for Boston and Canada. An escape tunnel ran under the intersection where traffic jams up today. If their luck held, if the fugitives evaded the bounty hunters in wait on the banks of the Raritan River ten miles to the north and got to the other side, then our neighborhood was their last stop before liberty. I think about that when I walk past the large yellow house, now an office, and imagine their voices praying as I walk to the bank.

I grew up thinking that New Jersey was part of the North; but Southern parents considered Princeton University the last "safe" school above the Mason Dixon line to send their sons with their servant slaves. Many guessed wrong. After four years of abolitionist professors, quite a few Southern sons freed their slaves, and three freed families settled on the other side of the quarry behind Evelyn Place, now a park. According to *The Princeton Recollector*, an oral history project in town, their descendants "belonged to the Jugtown 'Quick Steps' and would challenge the Pine Street Gang to games." One descendant, a generation or two after that, was key to integrating Princeton's public schools in 1947, the first New Jersey school system to formally do so. And, in another intersection of history, her daughter taught in the elementary school where my daughter started kindergarten.

Side Porch Sherry

At first, in 1970, our cul-de-sac seemed full of "old" ladies who were probably younger than I am now. There was Natasha, the widow of a famous mathematician, remarried to a New York composer. The James sisters next door with their white, white hair, curled tight. And Mrs. Kahler, with a heavy German accent, stooped and solemn-faced.

Only Barbara, Paul's wife, was under thirty like me when we moved in. Between us we had five kids under age seven, who would play Hide and Seek and Pop a Wheelie, while we sat under the ceiling fan on my side porch, drinking afternoon sherry. After two glasses, we didn't hear anything but our giggles, and that seemed fine (the cul-de-sac was pretty safe from cars and no one worried about strangers then). We'd sip and talk, feeling quite civilized, until there was a big shriek for help, or it was time to call in the gang, give baths, make dinner.

Barbara, nee Boggs, came from a well-known Southern political family; politics was in her blood. With her quick wit and irresistible smile, she soon became freeholder and then mayor. Which meant our street was plowed first when it snowed. Even better was the can-do energy she infused in everyone: to be an upbeat community. Benches started appearing everywhere, and we became outdoor people who walked, biked and sat in outdoor cafes whenever it was over 55 degrees. Restaurants kept adding tables on their section of sidewalk, and we would have been dancing in the streets by now if Barbara had lived.

It happened so fast: a spot on the eye, melanoma, a black patch— until she added sequins, and then purple, red, and gold patches, one for every outfit. They made us smile, we got used to them, expected new bursts of her energy—and then she was gone. It seemed impossible. She was fifty-one and full of life, and she died when I, the one who had had breast cancer, was alive—and all around us, the elderly ladies thrived.

Natasha, until well into her eighties, took the New York bus on the corner to the Courant Institute to translate mathematics articles from Russian. Mrs. Kahler, high into her eighties, hitched a ride with us to New Hampshire. And the James sisters, late in their seventies, assured us at every Labor Day picnic how much they loved to hear Julie play the piano in spring when our windows were open.

Then one day, the James sisters were gone to separate nursing homes. By choice or necessity no one knew. Then Natasha died followed by Mrs. Kahler. Paul, Barbara's husband, became the oldest on the street, with Stu next in line until Dick and Scotia moved across the street. Dick, a filmmaker, is five years older than Stu and hauling his video equipment in and out of his van daily. Very reassuring, as are Barbara's wooden benches. There are five on the way to the center of town, and Stu and I stop to sit on them, especially when a red-and-purple sunset lights the whole sky above town: Barbara's favorite colors.

The White Picket Fence

What was once the Kahler house, first one on the right, now has a white picket fence. It looks cheerfully Americana, defining boundaries with slats open enough to see into, but not enter without unhinging the gate. The rest of the street sprawls as before, one yard spilling into the next with scattered hedges here and there.

I rebel against the fence as I do to any change of my landscape that I didn't initiate, including each leaf that falls after we rake. "So we'll rake them again!" Stu says with equanimity; but he also accepts the giant maple falling over in the last hurricane, its top branch landing inches from our front door. And the holly trees that were Mr. Mackle's "perfect specimens"—he'd made a special trip to Connecticut for them—are now giants with arms joined to block the light, creating a muddy tunnel to reach the side yard. We should have pruned them, we learned too late: after the tree roots sapped the soil nutrients and killed the grass, according to the gardener. He suggests bluestone steps to cross the mud, and Stu says, "Sure, why not? Let the next owner tackle the mud."

I want our yard as it was when Mr. Mackle took us around, giving us Latin names to every prized bush and tree before he allowed us inside. We joked he would give us a test before we could buy the house, but barely listened, assuming his perfection would stay as is. Every generation seems to think of "now" being forever. My grandchildren assume the white picket fence has always been there, and even their parents forget that it wasn't. So they don't look for dips and chips as I do, waiting for what feels permanent to be gone.

Furniture for Sale

Albert Einstein used to visit our street. So did Thomas Mann and other European intellectuals who, fleeing Hitler in the 1930s, resettled in Princeton to start again at the Institute for Advanced Study. They gathered in Erich Kahler's house on the corner—dark brown then and no picket fence—to discuss history, politics, art, and literature, as if talk might soothe the wounds of dislocation and loss.

Or so I imagine from the way my father and uncles gathered in each other's living rooms in Queens, talking about leather business strategies, family gossip, and money troubles as I grew up. They fled Hitler as farm boys-turned-businessmen and never went beyond high school. I doubt they heard of Erich Kahler's *Man the Measure* or Hermann Broch's *The Death of Virgil* (Broch lived for years in the Kahler house) in their efforts to rebuild the comfort of their lives with conversation.

Erich Kahler died the year before we moved to Evelyn Place. All we knew is that Mrs. Kahler was his housekeeper, and then his wife. *How clever of her!* we thought for twenty years, filling in narrative gaps with a "duped-old-man" plot. We were wrong, I learned when reading Eileen Simpson's memoir, *Poets in Their Youth*. She and her husband, the poet John Berryman, had spent many evenings in the Kahler living room. She describes the salon for displaced scientists, economists, mathematicians, and musicians in this way:

> One stepped off a Princeton street and was plunged into Europe. Erich, dressed in a well-worn velvet smoking jacket, pulled back the portieres on a room in which a circle of chairs had been arranged around a large oval table. On its inlaid surface had been set out a crystal decanter of sherry, Bavarian wineglasses and a plate of Viennese cakes baked by Lili . . . a Viennese art historian who later became his wife.

So much for our invented, dime-store plots. If not for Hitler, Mrs. Kahler would have had a seat at Erich's table as art historian. As a refugee, and female, she had to take what she could get and, like my father, she made it work—as caretaker, lover, housekeeper, wife, and widow. She had grit, unwilling like so many others to live on memories of what had been lost.

For years, Mrs. Kahler would call our son to mow her lawn. "I vant to speak to Alan!" she'd screech into the phone, and because she was demanding and didn't pay well, he'd often disguise his voice: "Sorry, Alan is not at home." This was before we learned of Mrs. Kahler's past; but even after we knew, we'd joke about her—until a Viennese friend who had known the young Lili in Europe scolded me: "Lili is an amazing woman! Yes, she's harsh. But she is honest. And she has always been a true friend."

Mrs. Kahler lived into her midnineties, taking in boarders who also did chores, like her lawn. Twice in one month, she fainted and refused to let the Rescue Squad take her to the hospital. It looked as if she were destined for a nursing home, but Lili Kahler had other ideas. She placed an ad in the newspaper for a furniture sale, put neatly labeled prices on all Erich's Old World furniture—the inlaid table, the giant mahogany armoires and sideboard—and invited her niece to come up from Washington DC for the weekend. The niece found her aunt dead upstairs (lots of pills, we heard) while downstairs would-be buyers of antique furniture lined up at the front door.

Many are shocked by this story, but I find her gutsy. No quiet little old lady, she, willing to be ignored as if she weren't there. When, at eighty-eight, she asked to hitch a ride to New Hampshire, we thought *Six hours with her in the car, talking* and considered sneaking off in the middle of the night, taking the train, canceling our plans altogether. But with Mrs. Kahler, "No" was not an option. We took her round-trip two years in a row. We listened to her battles to get a street light on the corner and the difficulties of compiling Erich's letters for Princeton University, and tried to feel generous about helping the old.

Now the older I get, the more generous I feel to the Mrs. Kahlers, wondering if I were alone, what I'd do if someone, against my will, called 911 for me.

Sheepskin Rug

I'm not sure where we got it, probably from a friend of my father's who also made leather. The sheepskin was white and soft, maybe four feet by six feet, and didn't smell of farmyard like the large cowhide rug did, so it landed on our screen porch. I put the sheepskin in our bedroom, on my side of the bed, and liked stepping onto its soft assurance morning and night. Our son, at the time besieged by nightmares of robbers climbing the back stairs, found it to be a perfect refuge, so for months or longer, I'd have to pay attention not to step on him.

We had a carpet beneath the fur, wall-to-wall blue, but it was the sheepskin between my toes that soothed and fortified. I miss it—and have ever since we sold it in a garage sale in the late 1980s. We, then in our forties, decided to make some extra cash by getting rid of things lying around, like a useless rug.

We made $575 at that sale and felt triumphant. All that junk. A collapsible coat rack that I miss whenever we have a party. My grandmother's two teacups I miss whenever I open the dining room cupboard for good dishes (not too often). Five lace tablecloths from my grandfather's store in Stuttgart, way too much trouble to iron. The claw-footed bathtub. Wooden skis and dollhouses. The sheepskin rug.

That junk feels like lost history. Pieces of our past sold for $5 to $50, and we should do it again, get rid of more. That's what we keep vowing: another garage sale. It makes total sense until I step out of bed onto a rough, flat rug.

The Back Deck

The deck in the garden is rotting and we debate: Should we bother to fix it? We don't use it that much. The trouble, or maybe the good thing, is when we look at rotting boards, we feel rotten. Peeling paint and the leak seeping through the den ceiling from the upstairs bathroom have the same effect. They are extensions of the achy shoulder, the bad knee, and the shorter breath climbing to the third floor.

So we repair, repaint and rebuild. Not with the optimism we had redoing the kitchen after Stu's heart attack and my breast cancer. The breakfast nook of 1990, with its glass walls, sunlight, and garden view, has warmed us every day since then. Still, we say yes to the deck, telling ourselves that *if* we sell the house (we never say *when*), rotted planks would make potential buyers wonder what other rot is hidden. Our thirty-something carpenter recommends using cedar "that will last another fifty years," which makes us look at each other and laugh. Pressure-treated pine is just fine.

Becoming History

We start with a bookcase in half a room on the third floor. I say "half" because the eaves make the other half impossible to stand in. This was once the Moon Room, painted a royal blue with silver stars and a yellow moon to shine above our children as they played. It is now the Computer Room with built-in files angled into the space where you can't stand straight.

Two bookcases line the one normal wall, filled with travel books, shoeboxes of slides, my parents' 16-millimeter films, and hundreds of loose and framed photos from my mother's apartment. It's the perfect place to sort our lives, so our children don't throw out the relics with the clutter.

Stu takes down two dozen manila folders of clippings from the *New York Times Travel* section: Montreal 1973. Paris 1985. Those yellowed, crinkly articles can surely be dumped into the large plastic bag, one of many we plan to fill. Two hours is what we've allotted ourselves to start us off.

Stu begins piling articles next to the plastic bag. "What are you doing?" I ask.

"I want to check these out before I throw them away."

"They are easily twenty years old!"

"There may be some good restaurants. I'll call a few phone numbers."

I know better than to argue and begin taking guidebooks off the bookshelf: Egypt 1987; California 1973; Boston 1969; Rome 1986. I feel the same "You-never-know-when" allure and keep Egypt, giving up the rest.

We fill up two bags, half-pleased, half-guilty that it wasn't six. We'll do the basement next, we say. Old paints, dead batteries, bins of old wood, broken radios, and coffeepots will be easy to throw away. This fall maybe—or next spring.

I write this in my study, surrounded by books. Surely I can give away the ones I never liked and the yellow-paged paperbacks that crumble in my hands. But so many are very old friends—Austen, Tolstoy, Flaubert, Montaigne, Marjorie Morningstar—who hold the girl who filled their margins with ideas about love, destiny, and contradiction. My son says, "Why buy print books with the library down the street? Anyway, Kindle has bigger font." I agree totally and don't try to explain why new versions of old favorites are in front of my old copies.

Sturdy Illusions

I noticed a small hole on our front lawn the other day. I tried to fill it, but the dirt kept disappearing. I mentioned it to the guys who mow the lawn, and yesterday, on my way to tennis, late as usual, they called me over. "I'm in a rush," I said, but they kept motioning. I came closer and saw that the little hole had become one foot in diameter, deep and dark.

One man had a flashlight, and when I leaned over, there was a giant chamber, eight feet wide and eight feet deep, under more than half our front lawn. The upper walls were made of brick, the lower were made of mud and rocks. I was flabbergasted. All those years of feeling safe running across the grass, thinking we lived on a sturdy piece of history, and it could have caved in any minute! It happened to Paul, I learned later. He'd been walking on the floor of a shed behind his house, and the floorboards collapsed under him. He fell into a similar hole, he told me, but fortunately his son David heard his calls and got him out with a ladder.

What were these chambers? I imagined the Underground Railroad. I imagined the Horner factory basement; the bricks looked like those kinds of bricks. The town engineer said it was an old septic tank, but we weren't sure. Maybe we should call the Historical Society; it could be something amazing, we thought, until reality set in. There could be a huge hole in front of our house for months, years maybe. We'd have to sell the house with the hole. The engineer is right, we decided, and the gardener filled the chamber with seven truckloads of stone.

Now you can't see a thing, whatever is down there. Whoever buys our house will, like us, be drawn to its solid square shape, its sturdy white pillars, and all the possibilities of the past they evoke.

A Trunk of Surprise

The day after we moved onto Evelyn Place, we found an old steamer trunk in the attic, made for ocean voyages and big enough to hide in. And that's what Don Moore did. It was at a party we gave a month later for our former neighbors at Glen Acres, a U-shaped street of fifteen houses surrounded by fields outside town. We had lived there from 1966 to 1970 before moving into downtown Princeton with its sidewalks to everywhere. We liked the convenience, but we missed the Glen Acres neighborhood spirit—and friends like Don and Ruth Moore, and their twins (our kids' favorite babysitters).

The Moores lived in the same ranch house model we'd had, three houses down. They were original owners, one of five African American families to buy in this planned interracial community, one of two built in New Jersey in 1957 by Morris Milgram, a Philadelphia developer who believed, "If we don't learn to live together soon, the world is going to come apart."

Don was a sales manager; Ruth, a social worker—and they knew all things house. We knew nothing—this was our first house—so whenever the skylight leaked or the pipes froze, Don, handsome and generous, came over with can-do advice and the promise of a perfect martini after or during the project (depending on how long it took). His high spirits made me, and everyone else, have fun for the hell of it.

Which was why, when Don opened the steamer trunk at our party and said, "Ssshh, I'm going to hide," I laughed, ready for fun. In he went, the lid went down, and when the rest of the party walked in with Stu (he'd been giving his house-history tour), I said, "Here is our ghost room!" and Don jumped out: "Surprise!" That no one had a heart attack still amazes me, but we were younger then. All that day we laughed. And after that, we kept reminiscing *Remember when Don jumped out of the trunk?* always with a chuckle.

We wouldn't have met the Moores or the Drewrys, or our other African American neighbors, if Stu hadn't seen the four-by-six-inch card "For Sale By Owner" on the Princeton University bulletin board. We had been house hunting in a rush because Stu had to return to the University of Michigan and defend his thesis; his Princeton job depended on it. We had almost settled for a split-level that edged close to a ravine—"ideal for a young family with two small children," according to our realtor! Thankfully, we discovered our red-and-brown ranch house, full of light and enough bedrooms, affordable, and on a street where our kids could be safe riding a bike or tricycle.

"Why didn't you show them *that* house?" we heard our realtor's boss shout, as we left their office after informing them that we bought independently, so no commission. Her defense, which we heard as we walked down the hall: "I didn't think they'd want to move into *that* neighborhood." That took us by surprise. We couldn't have come across as bigots or snobs. We supported the growing civil rights movement but didn't buy the house out of idealism. It was because we loved it, the university gave us a mortgage, and an interracial neighborhood was not a minus but a plus. We hadn't been marching, we weren't Freedom Riders, but we could buy this house.

One-third of Glen Acres' families were black, and everyone wanted to keep it that way. You felt it in the air, every day, as a dozen kids, ages four to twelve, black and white, roamed from house to house, checking butterflies at the Pecks', playing kickball, Bombardment, or tag on the grass near the Duncans', with everyone looking out for every child—and feeding them! You could get a peanut butter and jelly sandwich at any house; even our little Alan knew that.

Growing up in Queens, I knew only white kids, mostly Jewish. At college, I lived across the hall from Addie and Denny, who grew up in very Waspy Grosse Pointe and had never met a Jew. We became comfortable enough with each other so that one night that first semester, sitting around in pajamas, drinking beer, Addie asked shyly, "Do Jews ever have horns?" And I answered "No!" more with amusement than insult.

The one African American in our dorm, Linda White, had a single on the top floor—and kept to herself. We talked, but never laughed with the ease I had with Don Moore whenever I'd meet him on his nightly street "patrol" with Loki and Bimbo, his two poodles (one black, one white). I had no Linda stories to tell, as I had Don stories, like the one of his ringing the doorbell of a new white family that moved into Glen Acres. "Excuse me," he said. "I was using my bow and arrow, and one landed on your roof. Do you mind if I climb up to get it?" The neighbors, flummoxed, said the roof was high, dangerous, and Don laughed. "You're right. Come for a drink instead. I'm Don Moore." A lifetime friendship began along with another Don story to make you smile.

At the fiftieth anniversary celebration of Glen Acres, over a hundred people came—those who left, as we did, and those who stayed, plus some of the Fair Housing advocates who did battle with Princeton banks and realtors, afraid of falling house values. "We raised $165,000—huge in those days—and got a 17 percent return," said one of the original white activists from the podium on the grass. "We proved that integrated housing could be profitable!" The black pastor of the Witherspoon Street Presbyterian Church spoke of her church pride that this special neighborhood "where people took a chance on one another" was forged in the church meeting room below her office. This church, together with two white congregations, had spearheaded the move to build a community committed to tolerance.

The mayor of West Windsor, where Glen Acres kids went to school, said this neighborhood "represents the very best of human spirit and a triumph over the worst of human spirit." After that came praise for Helen Duncan's endless supply of brownies. "The best ever, as always."

The former mayor of Princeton—he had lived in Glen Acres before moving into town—thanked the neighborhood for making people pay attention to the possibilities of affordable, integrated housing in our area. "Every other project depended on what happened here." A bit self-congratulatory, but true. Glen Acres had continued to succeed, where Maplecrest, also built in 1957 by Morris Milgram, became all white. Maybe because it was built in town, close to the Princeton shopping center, without a buffer of isolated fields two miles away. Maybe because it didn't have the core of eight families, black and white, who stayed put—and were totally committed to interracial togetherness and that early utopian spirit.

Several of the gang of kids we'd known, now adults, came to the podium to talk about their amazing childhood and the disillusionment, afterward, of living in less accepting places: *Nowhere else came close!* They all, black and white, seemed to agree on that. A young woman who once loved our tree house said: "We were a bunch of color-blind kids having fun together . . . and it didn't matter how old you were, how athletic you were, whether a boy or girl, black, white, Jewish, Baptist. The only thing that interrupted us playing was the ice cream man's bell."

Another whose jazz music once filled the street said: "Growing up, I had no idea that this was a planned integrated community. I only found out reading an article a few years ago. Our parents never told us we were part of some special experiment."

And another, who said he'd just moved to New York City to escape the Midwest suburbs, said: "I moved twelve times in the last twenty-five years . . . trying to find another community like this. I thought there were Glen Acres all over the world. So it was a shock, after graduating Oberlin College, to move to another part of Ohio and find it was one of the most racially segregated communities in the country."

Then a new homeowner from Central America told of how grateful she was to "this special neighborhood." Soon after she moved in, her daughter had a chance to go to the Model UN in Washington DC. The school couldn't pay travel expenses, and the dozen merchants whom she wrote wouldn't pay. So the neighborhood—"You barely knew us!"—chipped in enough to cover the trip's cost. "Thank you all," she said in tears to more applause.

But what stayed with me most from that day was Don Moore's speech. It was a Don I didn't recognize. On the podium with no hint of a smile, he described how hard it was for Ruth and him to find decent housing in the early 1950s. He'd grown up in Princeton, living with a grandfather who had built and owned buildings in the downtown; yet that meant nothing. White homeowners sounded enthusiastic on the phone, "Yes, come take a look!" and then "No" after they saw the color of his skin. Don had a solid job, education, and a down payment, yet even his close friend reneged on renting an apartment to him because white tenants would object. "So what a shock it was for me to come here to Glen Acres and have someone, a white guy, say, 'Welcome! Let us show you around.'"

Don ended by saying how glad he was that the neighborhood had survived as intended—without tipping all white or all black, as the realtors predicted. And how grateful he was to this community where he and his wife, Ruth, could raise their children comfortably and, Ruth added afterward, "without worrying about the N word."

Over the years, the Moores enlarged their house, adding a family room of high, clerestory windows that let in more light and greenery. In fact, almost every original black family stayed—*Where would we find a better place?*—along with four of the original white families. "Our neighborhood has kept its balance," Don's voice cracked with emotion. "Thank God for that."

A moment of silence on the grass, and everyone cheered. The speeches over, kids started a ballgame while grown-ups began chatting. *How's it going? What's happening?* as families who returned for the day reconnected with those who never left.

I walked over to Don, eighty-five looking like sixty-five, to say how much his speech moved me. "I had no idea you'd had such a tough time!" I said, and immediately felt stupid. Because of course I knew. How could I not? I'd read plenty about discrimination, unfair housing practices, white flight—and yet, somehow, I'd disconnected that from Don, who helped to make me part of a color-blind life. What drew us together was not our differences, but what we shared as friends and neighbors. Like the stories he told of his Aunt Kissye, who owned a beauty salon in town, a black woman of force and sass. And of Uncle Gay, a physician, who was one of the first African Americans to graduate from Yale. I loved Don's pride and affirmation in the telling, the same pride I had telling how my family outwitted the Nazis, smuggling money out of the Third Reich taped to the backs of toilets on trains to Switzerland. I repeated that story often and never mentioned the one about my uncle's suicide after failing to restart his life in America.

On the grass, Don told everyone what was always there: the grave injustices hiding in plain sight. I had missed them, thinking not here, not in Glen Acres, not to confident, handsome Don who made blacks and whites laugh easily together. And so I left History behind—but of course it was waiting there.

Don and I hugged. We reminisced about how little Julie and Alan kept begging me to go somewhere so his Christine could babysit; how our collie, Karma, kept chasing every damn car. Then we chuckled about Don as the attic ghost. "Come over! We should make him reappear!" I said, thinking this time we'd try for the hard stories, still unshared.

"Absolutely," he said, the Don twinkle in his eyes, as if he were again raising the lid of the steamer trunk, ready to surprise.

What's a Rally to Do?

Overt anti-Semitism was my parents' old world, not mine. Yes, I'd hear an occasional remark, but everyone gets that in multiethnic New Jersey. No big deal—until 500 anti-Semitic flyers were posted on the walls and kiosks of the college where I had taught for twenty years. That was a shock. Some had swastikas leaning on Jewish stars. Some had a picture of Hitler and an Israeli soldier, both of equal size. The caption: "How many millions must die?" Some had the Christlike figure of crucifixion paintings, but instead of the expected cross, the arms were draped over a Jewish star, evoking the imagery of Jew as Christ killer. The caption: "Stop the Murder. Free the Palestinians."

"Anti-Semitism like that is gone now!" say students yearly in my "Holocaust through Literature and Film" course, while examining a Nazi flyer, circa 1934. It showed a black-haired, fat man with a long, hooked nose handing candy to two blond children, and the translated caption read: "Jewish sex fiend passes out sweets with sinister intent." People don't believe such rubbish anymore, according to most of the class, who tend to be white, Christian, early twentyish, first-generation college students.

They'd repeat this conviction (although more tentatively) after watching *The Long Walk Home*, a film about the African American bus boycott in Montgomery, 1955. And again (although with even less conviction) after *School Ties*, a movie set in a rich, New England prep school in the 1950s, where the kids turn against a newly imported football star once they find out (after a winning football season, their first) that he is Jewish.

I showed these movies interspersed with Holocaust films to connect past with present. Otherwise it was too easy to be self-righteous about what those Germans did way back when. Gradually, platitudes about tolerance gave way to personal stories about bigotry: from not being served as a black couple at Denny's after the prom, to picking on a Jewish roommate who hogged the refrigerator with kosher food, to shrugging off Polish jokes from fraternity brothers who didn't know you were Polish.

The initial storytellers were usually African American, Hispanic, or Jewish, but then everyone jumped in, sharing injustices they had observed, had been victim of or taken part in. Conversation would become less guarded. We'd argue about harmless joking vs. ugly prejudice, moral responsibility vs. risking your life, and what would we do next time it happened. Some minds were changed, some not; but as long as honesty mixed with civility, everyone kept listening to one another.

The 500 anti-Semitic flyers were taken down quickly (someone said they'd been posted "without going through school channels") and replaced by new flyers showing Palestinian women weeping for their sons, daughters, and lost land that was their birthright. They made a strong case for justice for the Palestinians and affirmed, to me, what free speech on a college campus should be about: the right to argue your position without the crutch of hate speech that prevents real listening to anything but insult.

An official rally was organized by the administration in response to the flyers as a way of saying communally: "Hey! You can't do that around here!!" Faculty received an email calling for a Rally for Harmony that was "intended to bring about a sense of unity between every member of the community." I expected good campus support from Jews and non-Jews, especially from my activist friends.

My second shock was when my friends on the political left decided to boycott the rally. The 500 flyers, they said, were a nonissue. The real issue was Israel as "The Occupier" with a totally unjustifiable policy. Citing the right of free speech, they were more upset with the college administrators, whom they accused of oppressing the students who posted the flyers, than with the students themselves. One colleague—and a friend of twenty years—said that taking the flyers down was an outrage, a conspiracy. (I suddenly heard *Jewish conspiracy.*) "All the flyers did was display Palestinian suffering," she said, practically spitting the words out. "So what if they didn't get official permission, a mere technicality, an excuse meant to appease the powers in the Holocaust program who initiated the rally." (I heard "Jewish power.") She wasn't going near the rally, which, she said, would be "totally controlled and scripted."

"But this rally at least admits to a college problem," I said, swallowing anger that felt dangerous. She shrugged. "You didn't find the flyers offensive?" No response. "The Jew as Christ-killer, the way the arms are out, as if nailed to a cross?"

Her eyes widened. "Gee, I didn't get that! I saw it as the figure in the Pieta, you know, a mother suffering for her dead son, like Palestinian mothers."

You are a professor whose walls are lined with history books. Are you really that naïve? I wanted to yell. *And what about Israeli mothers who are suffering?* The bell rang for the next class. "Well, many people feel the flyers are anti-Semitic," was all I said and backed away. *So this is why my dad left Germany!* I thought, hurrying off, my heels echoing on the red floor tile. *People like her, angry and unpredictable. People like me, diplomatically silent.*

"Okay, okay, so maybe I'm overreacting," I conceded, over lunch, to another friend, who dismissed my analogy to Nazi Germany as Jewish paranoia made worse by my parents' narrow escape. They left because my father saw the danger signs. I grew up on the story of how he'd attended a Hitler rally in 1932 and told my mother that night, "If that man gets elected, we leave!" It was told again and again, a survival guide of warning signs to look for, like these 500 "signs." Why weren't my friends seeing them?

"You can be against Israeli policy and not be an anti-Semite," said this colleague as we ate tuna sandwiches. Weaned on antiwar rallies of the sixties, he had been reenergized by what he saw as another version of the injustice of Vietnam: the military/industrial complex, First World capitalism vs. Third World poverty—now with Israel as the colonial oppressor. "The Israeli government has no credibility if it keeps building Jewish settlements on Arab land," he said quietly.

"No argument about that!" I replied. My concern for the security and safety of Israel didn't make me pro-settlements, a distinction that kept getting lost in the "for-or-against" polarization. Nor was I against saying that out loud, as if all criticism of Israel were subversive. The dangers of what *Tikkun* editor Rabbi Michael Lerner calls "Jewish PC" are as real as "Palestinian PC." "So are you coming to the rally?" I offered him my bag of chips as extra enticement, feeling we'd connected.

"No, it's a fraud."

"But not having a rally is worse."

"The flyers weren't anti-Semitic in intent, you know. One of the two kids who posted them was in Jewish Studies."

Would you say the same if Clarence Thomas, being black, voted against affirmative action? That makes it okay? I didn't say that, still hoping he would come. "If we don't support a harmony rally, the extremists rule—whatever their stand," I said. "You can't let hate control the political agenda."

He shook his head. "No one will say what he really thinks!" and stood up to go. "Besides," he added, turning to walk away, "I have a class, a review session." He waved.

"So bring them!" I called. His was a social history course, after all.

I headed for the rally, thinking about Saul Friedlander's book, *Nazi Germany and the Jews*. One of its main premises is that the early silence of the universities as a moral guardian of society helped to make Hitler feel he had a green light to proceed. I decided to send my colleague the quote that struck me most:

> When Jewish colleagues were dismissed, no German professor publicly protested; when the number of Jewish students was drastically reduced, no university committee or faculty member expressed any opposition; when books were burned throughout the Reich, no intellectual in Germany, or for that matter anyone else within the country, openly expressed any shame.[1]

I always wondered what German professors told themselves in order *not* to act. Was it some rationalized sense of justice that let them ignore the images of Jew as sex fiend, and was it the same impulse that let my colleagues give a pass to 500 flyers of Jew as Christ killer, unconcerned?

Only sixty or so (out of five thousand on campus) gathered for harmony in the D-Wing Circle on a blue-sky day before finals week. Students representing fourteen groups were there (including the Jewish Student Union, the Women's Coalition, the Asian Society, and the Muslim Association), as well as some administrators and a dozen or so faculty. Everyone else was either too busy with exams, didn't know about it, didn't care, or was boycotting like my friends. The college president didn't show, someone official said, "because of a delayed board meeting."

A Muslim student in T-shirt and jeans came to the open mic, saying, "We need to think of ourselves as human beings first, not as Jew, Christian, and Muslim first." Vigorous applause. A Jewish student with a yarmulke stood up to proclaim, "We are all God's children." More

---

1 Saul Friedlander, *Nazi Germany and the Jews* (New York: Harper Perennial, 1998), 60.

applause. An African American sorority president said, "We must overcome our differences and treat each other with respect." More applause. Then a man with a turban said, "We are all Americans who seek peace." More applause. No one cared that the words sounded like Hallmark cards, for we knew the alternative from other campuses: shouting, pushing, even fistfights. And how quickly, seven thousand miles away, the lack of commitment to these words of harmony had turned into the tragic spiral of Israeli/Palestinian violence.

A concrete wall surrounded the circle and on it were colored flyers—Civility, Freedom, Communication, Dignity, Respect—the kind you see in elementary school classrooms teaching virtue. For six-year-olds, they are vigorous words to be taken seriously. For adults, they are tired repetitions that make us impatient—yes, yes, yes, but . . .

But within the walled circle these words contained what might explode. A colleague who loves Plato and Aristotle came up to me and whispered, her face red with anger: "I'm here to support anyone who tells Israel to get the hell out of Palestine!"

"Hey, this is a Harmony Rally!" I swallowed *Jerk!*

"A waste of time," she said, and left. I thought how her anger, like mine, could turn the Rally for Harmony into a CNN Crossfire, where only yelling counts and people end up slinging slogans and epithets until all you can do is cheer or boo or change channels in disgust.

Platitudes such as "We must treat each other with respect" keep people civil—and connected, like saying, "I love you" on days when you feel the opposite. By themselves these words do little, except to ward off permanent damage; but without them, there is no chance to lay a foundation that might turn self-righteousness into something worth working on.

I was about to leave when my lunch friend, the activist, showed up. He was "only passing by," but wanted me to know that he was planning a series of *real* forums next semester to discuss the Middle East and its repercussions. He and another faculty member were already drawing up a list of speakers to lead discussions on the history of the region, American policy options, religious and cultural differences, Zionism vs. Racism, first amendment issues.

"Great!" I said, and thought if the atmosphere were right, I might try again to convince my colleagues of their blindness to those anti-Semitic flyers. And Muslim students might be more open about bigotry against them on campus. And we could debate free speech vs. hate speech and invite Palestinians and Israelis to tell personal stories, putting a human face on ideology. And if that happened on other campuses all over, maybe governments might . . .

I was on a roll of optimism, imagining a takeover of people becoming reasonable. But then the harmony rally, oxymoron that it is, ended, and someone began ripping down the bright pink, green, and yellow signs. *Stop! I'll take them!* I started to yell, knowing that wherever we meet, we'll need to hang Civility, Freedom, Respect, Dignity, and Reason—and to keep looking at them.

Close Call

Last time, I thought myself lucky. When I told the judge that I live in Princeton, am a writer and professor, and my mother had been held up at gunpoint in a parking garage, I soon heard, "Thank you for your services #6." End of jury duty. I planned to say all that again, but just in case, I asked a friend who is a retired New Jersey prosecutor: "What outfits did you definitely reject in jury selection?" I was thinking high black books, artsy vest, black beret tipped over my eyebrows—something ultraliberal and slightly kooky. "People often call to find out how to avoid jury duty, but you're the first to ask me what to wear!" She laughed as if I had told a bad joke—and gave nothing away. I was clearly on my own.

At 8:45 a.m. I huddle with twenty other latecomers under the Juror Shuttle Bus sign in a parking lot that is next to the highway running through Trenton, the state capital. We are young and old, black, white, Asian, Hispanic, fat, thin, running late, and sleepy. Someone says, "It's not too far to walk," but no one moves. This group—we hail from nearby suburbs and towns—would rather be late than risk unknown urban streets, even if the sun is out, the air crisp, and we will soon be late.

A white bus with "County Sheriff" printed on its side finally rolls up to drive us through narrow streets with red brick sidewalks, old enough to have been here when Washington crossed the Delaware on Christmas Eve, surprising the drunken Hessian soldiers. That was 1776, and the Battle of Trenton, fought right here, saved our fledgling democracy from King George's tyranny. Today I see darkened bars, three men talking at a corner, a few boarded-up stores, and a half-lit diner.

The bus stops at the Mercer County Courthouse, and with juror badges in hand as instructed, we follow the guards, prisonerlike, up well-worn stone steps, through a security turnstile, down a long hall, and into a cavernous room filled with two hundred other prospective jurors (they'd arrived on time).

A blond woman cheerfully announces "plenty of coffee." An African American man dressed in a blue uniform plays a video about what to expect and how lucky we are to live in a country that has trial by jury. In high school we snickered at such earnestness, but that was the complacent fifties. In today's uncertain world, I feel a twinge of guilt as I touch my tipped beret and try to ignore an annoying voice in my head: "It's time to put up or shut up!"

Because, yes, I am one of those who rail every morning at the *New York Times'* headlines: *Where are the middle-of-the-roaders? Why don't they stand up to those who usurp decency and respect?* I'm loud enough for Stu to wait upstairs until I reach the Style section or Science Tuesday before descending to the kitchen.

My sociologist friend Suzanne likes to say: "The silent majority isn't called silent for nothing." A child of 1930s Austria, she worries about rising fascism, as do many I know, myself included, with personal connections to Europe in those years. It could happen here, they warn, and not just to Jews or gays or Jehovah's Witnesses, but to everyone deemed "Other" by those on a rant that "the real America" is lost.

The real America is in this room. They come in every accent, class, and color, some in suits, some in ripped jeans, one with white vampire nails, many with tattoos, a few in pale silk saris, one in a red print muumuu. We read, talk quietly, text and knit. The young Chinese woman beside me is sewing a Gingerbread Boy potholder. I'm struck by the collective orderliness and willingness to cooperate, as if what is happening here matters.

The next trial is a criminal trial, the blond woman announces: "So no early dismissal. The judge wants all of you for possible jury selection." The room is abuzz. What if it is a murder trial? That could mean weeks or more. Some rush to the clerk's desk with excuses, and I debate and calculate—Bad back? Surgery? Perjury? But I line up, as most of us do, to climb the stairs to Judge N's courtroom. "There is an elevator for those who need it," says the man in blue uniform, but four flights of steps may well be my exercise for the day.

We sit on benches like pews, elbows touching in a stately, wood-paneled courtroom. I'm squeezed between a Skull and Bones T-shirt and an argyle sweater as framed portraits of solemn men in black robes look down from the walls.

"All rise for the judge!" says a booming voice, and a man enters and seats himself on a highly polished wooden throne above us. He has a white Santa beard, round face, and rosy cheeks, and I imagine him saying, "Ho, ho, ho!" in other circumstances. But today he is briefing us on the charges: the defendant, a prisoner at Trenton State Prison, is accused of aggravated assault on two prison guards. (The name Trenton State means nothing to me, but it houses the worst of the worst, I find out posttrial from my prosecutor friend—one of many facts we won't learn in this courtroom.)

We are handed the Jury Questionnaire, and the judge says he will ask all twenty-eight questions during jury selection, and we must pay close attention to everyone's answers. "So no cell phones, no reading," the judge says cheerfully. "Otherwise a long process will become a long, long process." He starts reading and seems in no hurry: "A juror must be 18 or older, a citizen, able to read and understand English . . ." I reconsider the possibilities of my bad back: that I *will* be disabled, sitting for hours on these benches. I imagine everyone else thinking the same thing.

I am in seat #13 in the jury box, which is soft-padded at least. My number was among the first called, but dozens have come and gone while I sit here. My funky look isn't working. Only people in seats #1 and #6 keep being questioned and replaced.

The judge asks everyone: "Is there anything about the length or scheduling of the trial that would interfere with your ability to serve?" The answers come back, "I have a business trip." Excused. "I have nonrefundable cruise tickets for our anniversary." Excused. "I'm having dental surgery next week." Excused.

"This judge is really easy," whispers the guy in seat #12. He's been beside me for two hours, a churchy type in white shirt and bow tie who, it turns out, writes for the *Wall Street Journal.* "Last time I sat in a jury box," he says, "if you told the judge you had a business trip or cruise, he'd tell you to change it. Not this judge." He is letting anyone with a reasonable excuse go: A mother caring for three young children and a sick mother. Excused. A young man starting a new job who is worried his absence will make a bad first impression. Excused.

I look to see which questions might get me off. *Have you or any family member ever been a victim of a crime?* Aside from my mom's mugging, I could mention the thief who swiped my handbag near Macy's and the flasher I saw when I was nine, on the corner near P.S. 3. The police made me come to the station to identify the man in a lineup, which I did. I was never sure he did it, or that he'd been locked up, and kept looking for him near that street corner.

Do you think that a police officer is more likely or less likely to tell the truth than any other witness . . . ? At least fifteen people are dismissed on this one, and I, in good conscience, could answer "Less likely" and go home. But when my turn comes, I keep quiet. Five hours into the process, I've become hooked on who will stay, who will go, and what will happen next. The shirker me has given way to the citizen—and the writer easily hooked on stories.

Some dismissals are easy to predict: an unemployed janitor, a guy arrested on a protest march for wearing a mask, a woman whose family is full of cops, a scary-looking white guy who storms in and storms out. The defense lawyer eliminates the conservatives; the prosecutor, the liberals. And both say good-bye, as one lawyer friend put it, "to all who think too much and think they know too much." Last time I was called that meant writers, lawyers, social workers, and professors; but this time we are still here. So is the woman who said her hobby is gambling in Atlantic City and another who, when the judge asked why she'd make a good juror, answered: "God will tell me the truth!"

It's after 5 p.m. before we have a full jury, and we can't leave until the judge finishes his instructions: No talking to anyone. No researching this case on the Internet. Remember, "You are the sole judges of the facts!" and must base decisions "only on the testimony of witnesses and on objects that are exhibits admitted in the courtroom." We are sworn in on the Holy Bible—*What about separation of church and state?*—and told to report back at 9 a.m. sharp.

Thirteen of us sit at a long table in a narrow juror room, waiting for the judge to call us to his courtroom. It's 9:20 a.m. and #14 is not here yet, so the trial can't begin. Two of us will be alternates, and a lottery will decide, says our guard, but either way, no one is excused from the proceedings, so I'd rather be one of the voting twelve.

I'm next to a white guy, 300 pounds easy, with a dragon tattoo on his forearm and smiley face buttons on his T-shirt. A cartoonist by night, he whips out his cell phone to show me his best character: an orange monster, huge and a little menacing, but something sweet in him too, like this guy. On my other side is a fortyish African American studying stock reports; he's a broker for Merrill Lynch.

Across the table is the insurance claims officer with whom I walked from the parking lot. We both chose fresh air over the juror bus and arrived triumphant with exercise on streets that proved safe. I'd always pictured claims officers as Scrooge, but he is a cherub-faced, young music lover whose girlfriend likes yoga.

Over lunch and during breaks, I talk to the perky Hispanic woman who works in a state office in Trenton, helping the poor get heat. (She's the one who told the judge her hobby was gambling). A perfectly coiffed African American woman, who is a branch manager for Bank of America, is reading George H. Bush's memoir during breaks and recommends it. The born-again Christian divorcee who told the judge, "God will tell me the truth" talks about her new partner, a female corrections officer. The Jewish lawyer, retired from Port Authority, says he would have been in the Twin Towers on 9/11 if Mayor Giuliani hadn't called an uptown meeting that morning. The Protestant psychologist, a single mom with three kids, says she loves her college job in Philadelphia. And my jury box mate, the *Wall Street Journal* reporter, has left his suit at home and returned in jeans and a sweatshirt. His failed "outfit" of yesterday also discarded.

The missing juror, an East Asian woman, arrives fifteen minutes late, saying she had to drop her daughter at school before coming here. "No bathroom breaks for you!" someone calls out in an easy manner that makes her smile. I decide this crazy mix of people—half men, half women, seven white, four African American, two Hispanic, and one East Asian—will click as the kind of jury I wouldn't mind if I were on trial. It's a gut feeling, the same one I have when I walk into a new class and know, within five minutes, whether it will be a good semester or not.

Back in jury seat #13, I listen to the judge introduce the defense and prosecution teams. They are all sitting sideways to us, like silhouettes; the judge as well. The prosecutor is the trim white guy in a pinstriped suit next to a big black man with a bouncer's build. I assume he is the defendant, but he turns out to be the assistant prosecutor. So much for my liberalism, free from bias! The defense lawyer, a young white woman with a brown braid, is next to the defendant, a scrappy-looking white guy in his fifties, staring straight ahead as if catatonic. Maybe it's because his lawyer is wearing a suit with a mini-miniskirt that ends high on her thighs. All I can see are long, bare legs sitting close to a guy from jail.

The prosecutor opens first. He is smooth, practiced, and very high-tech. He shows us tons of photos of the prison layout, the five-by-eight-foot cell, the hallway outside the cell, the bolted-down bed and the toilet, which is in the middle of the room, and the cluttered wall-shelf, full of cruddy food. The defense lawyer clutches her notes during her opening statement, stumbling over words. She never looks at us. This must be her first trial.

The judge keeps warning us to pay attention only to admissible courtroom evidence. Here's what's presented as fact: The prison guard came to do a routine strip search. *Stripping is routine?* The prisoner cooperated until the guard decided to search his room for a lid from a soup can, a potentially dangerous weapon. *So why are can openers sold in the prison store?* The officer asked the inmate to find it, and after a few minutes, he heard, "Find it yourself, asshole!" The officer made him face the wall, and the defendant suddenly swung around and punched him in the shoulder. A second guard came in, and both guards fought the inmate, pinning him to the floor in the hallway outside the cell.

I'm on board, mostly, until the first prison guard, Witness #1, is called to the stand. The guy is six feet, weighs 325 pounds and looks like a bully. Why would someone half the size go after this guy? True, the prisoner looks creepy and could have a short fuse if baited. But I need context: Did the guy fight anyone else before? Did the guard have other complaints against him?

Answers keep getting cut off by "Objection" and "Sustained" and endless trips to the sidebar, where the judge and lawyers keep conferring. It's as if no one wants us to know who these people were before this moment. I think of the old days of American trials, at least in the Westerns I grew up watching. People knew everyone: the defendant, the family, and the witnesses. Your reputation was on trial with you.

During break, I wonder why there's a trial at all. The bank manager told me, as we stood in line for the bathroom, that the defendant is not getting out of jail no matter what. I had missed that fact—and am relieved. He's the kind given wide berth and no eye contact on a New York City subway.

Witness #1 took a seven-month disability leave after the incident to have rotator cuff surgery. From one punch? He probably tripped over the toilet in the middle of the room, and a heavy guy like him would fall hard. He says he never hit the prisoner, and "it was more like wrestling." He and the other guard needed to maintain order by pinning him down "until reinforcements came." *Really?*

The defense lawyer, in cross-examination, makes sure we know that the defendant is five foot eight and reminds the guard that he had been taking Motrin for his shoulder for months before the incident. She shows him the report. "I forgot about that," he says, his cheeks reddening. Maybe she is cleverer than she appears.

The officer says he doesn't know what the prisoner's original crime was—and his whole face turns red. She points out that strip searches are supposed to take place only in the shower room, but doesn't push it. Still, she is doing better. I'm definitely moving towards a strong "reasonable doubt." Especially when she asks, "Why didn't you search for the lid rather than ask the prisoner to do it?" and he answers, "I didn't want to cut myself." *Baloney.*

The prosecutor calls Witness #2, the second guard, and he's even bigger—six foot three and 347 pounds, the defense attorney slips in. Even a crazy guy wouldn't assault these two together. This guard looks nicer, not someone who would throw a first punch, more like a follower. He has also been out months on disability, three months for a bum knee. Unrelated, the prosecutor says. *Our tax dollars at work?* No surprise that his story matches the first guard's. They'd stand together, one story for two. I guess I should have checked yes on Question #16 about my police bias.

The defense lawyer starts Day 2 with a bad cold. She spends the judge's opening remarks sipping a row of tiny paper cups of water and carefully sniffling into fresh Kleenex she keeps taking out of her desk. Pay attention, I want to shout, glad that her legs are in black tights today. Her actions don't affect the defendant, who sits stone-faced and rigid as before, his eyes straight ahead except for one long glance our way, enough to make me look down, my heart racing.

Another prisoner, two cells away, is called to the stand. A small guy with graying Afro braids, he's been in this prison forever on five convictions, armed robbery mostly; but I like him better than the defendant. The defense lawyer does well establishing that he uses can lids for ashtrays and chopping tuna fish—and has never been asked about lids or strip-searched.[1] She also lets us know that the photos the prosecutor showed of the cell with the crusted food weren't of this prisoner's cell. She is really scoring until she asks, "Do you have any reason to lie?" Even I, who never watches courtroom TV, know better. Objection. Rephrased: "What kind of relationship do you have with the guard?" Does she really think he'll say, "He stinks!" and return safely to his cell for a long life?

---

1 From my prosecutor friend posttrial: "If you think cops stick together, what about prisoners? Oh my God!"

Next is the defendant who, I see, has dark, piercing eyes when he occasionally looks our way. He doesn't seem stupid. He is like a coiled spring despite a flat voice with no affect, as if he's on Thorazine. He says he never insulted anyone, never provoked an officer, never hit or made a swing in any way. When they hit him, he just curled up in a fetal position on his bed until he blacked out, woke up and blacked out again. Somehow, in between, he managed to squeeze out from under these two big guys and into the hall. He could hardly breathe let alone walk. Yet two hours later the video shows him doing both without much trouble.

I am feeling as I did at twenty-three, serving on the only other jury I've been on. A boy was on trial for drunken driving: Was he guilty or not? I listened to one side, then the other, and had no idea. Everyone seemed to be lying; everyone seemed to be telling the truth. I can't even remember the verdict.

"This was a cover-up!" says the defense lawyer in closing argument. She has more spirit, more confidence, insisting that the lapses in the defendant's memory come from the heat of the moment. Who remembers a crisis in exact detail?

I relate to that better than to the prosecutor's assertion that "any reasonable person would believe the police." Not these guys. Plus he shows endless photos and a video of the defendant getting off the bed, moving through the hall, etc. It reminds me of students whose papers rely on fancy font to hide lack of content. He doesn't address what will become a big question later: how a left-handed defendant could punch the guard with his right hand.

The judge, who really seems to want justice to work, takes an hour for his instructions on the law. He reminds us again to judge only the facts and that our verdict must factor in "beyond a reasonable doubt." And he stresses that we should not be prejudiced against a prisoner because he is a prisoner. We still don't know what he did or the length of his sentence. The judge spends twenty minutes explaining the charge of aggravated assault: that it must "purposely, knowingly, or recklessly cause bodily harm." Pain, he emphasizes, is an important component of bodily harm.

"There's no way a five-foot-eight guy weighing 158 can fight two 300-pounders in a small space," says the cartoonist. We are back in the jurors' room, trying to decide what is true. "A right-handed punch from a left-hander just wouldn't happen!" This from the blond psychologist mom who, it turns out, does boxing as a hobby. The insurance claims guy agrees: "You can't swing with your left hand and hit a right shoulder when your back is to the wall." This reminds me of Atticus in *To Kill a Mockingbird*, arguing that Tom was innocent because he was left-handed. It's also a common motif in movie and TV trials, so the argument is familiar, and we nod. "Which wall was it?" someone asks, and we look at the photos in evidence. Nothing seems obvious.

The bank manager notes how red the officer's face got during questioning and how defensive he seemed. The women nod; we notice such things. Except for the born-again Christian who counters: "I got red like that in my divorce proceedings. He was at fault, but I blushed." She blushes now, holding her ground.

The state worker returns to where we've been drifting: "I don't believe anyone is telling the truth." Lots of nods now. That's bad for the prosecutor who argued there was only one Truth, the officers' truth. The lawyer who worked in the Twin Towers says he has reasonable doubts. "The State did not make its case."[2] More nods about that. Nobody sympathizes with the prisoner, but where is the case? We should have seen a detailed medical report. The nurse, listed as a witness, was never called. Why not? Was there little bruising or a lot?

---

2 Another posttrial enlightenment: There may have been an informant who triggered the strip search, but no prosecutor could mention that or the guy would be killed.

We discuss the defense lawyer's incompetence, how she should have asked more about strip searches. How often are they done? And more about the missing lid. How often does this happen?

We wonder why the judge kept blocking information about the prisoner. Someone mentions reading about a judge in the Midwest who allowed makeup to cover tattoos on the defendant's face and neck because one was a swastika.

"I don't think that is fair. The defendant owns it."

"But he shouldn't have to incriminate himself."

"Okay. Then what about a big nose, brown skin, a pregnant belly? Where does it end?"

We are listening to each other, trying to understand, convince, sort out—and do the right thing. This is democracy at work, what the Battle of Trenton was all about: that the people's law, not a tyrant, gets to decide. George Washington would be pleased.

Someone asks for an informal reading of how people feel. The foreman, a bland man who got the job because he ended up in jury seat #1, agrees. We go around the table. Everyone feels there is reasonable doubt until we get to the born-again divorcee whose new partner is a corrections officer. "I believe the police."

"Tell us why."

"These guys are in prison for a reason. You can't trust them. The officers work hard, get paid, and hold a steady job. They are the ones to believe."

Silence. We don't know what to say. This is exactly what the judge warned against: making judgments because someone is in prison. I mention that, gently. Others second me, softly. But it is the African American bank manager at the other end of the table who looks directly at her and says firmly: "I think you are being prejudiced." There are gasps, but also relief at her civil directness. "You said, 'these guys,'" she continues with no sign of a sneer. "That means you are including everyone in the same category. I think that is prejudice."

Her words echo a history of racism that still defines the streets we avoid in Trenton. And yet, by being spoken in this little room, they mutate somehow. There's equality here: a black woman is confronting a white woman, without rancor or fear, about justice. And irony too: that the rights of a creepy white prisoner should not be prejudged. The Born Again is taken aback. The two have eye contact, but no darts of anger. She doesn't answer.

We continue around the table, ending with the foreman who affirms the reasonable doubt argument. What to do now? The lawyer asks the Born Again to say more, defend her position. "I can live with 'reasonable doubt,'" she whispers. Is it group pressure? The desire to go home? Over lunch, this woman had strong ideas about Cirque du Soleil. "It's not bells and whistles, just talent," she said passionately. "Everyone should go and see it." But she offers no other defense for a guilty verdict—and if she did, would we have listened?

Our verdict is "Not Guilty." No one is elated, as if we saved an innocent man from injustice. No one liked the guy. But we are collectively pleased with how we worked together as citizens: with civility and in good faith. And we go back to our lives feeling sensible and conscientious.

That night I google the defendant's name, something we couldn't do before. There he is in a Jersey Shore newspaper, his picture looming large on the front page. He is a handyman who molested small children in his clients' homes and posted videos of them on the Internet. I feel soiled, like the crud on the prison shelf. Was this what our twelve citizens contributed to American justice? To judge a child molester innocent? That he stays in jail is not enough comfort. I picture us in the jurors' room had we known. Reason and sensibility would have been out the window. No wonder the judge held the facts back. He was following Oliver Wendell Holmes's assessment: This is a court of law, young man, not a court of justice!

The guards probably knew what the guy did and beat him up, which would make our verdict correct. By law. And maybe we need The Law most for the ugly cases like this one. Old West vigilantism—Just shoot or hang them!—was simpler and cheaper, but "them" were often innocent, the ones powerless and marginalized in a community that didn't like blacks, Native Americans, drifters, immigrants, mentally disabled, atheists, whoever. Twelve people like us in a jury room were their one defense, preserving, however imperfectly, what Washington fought for down the street—or, rather, fought against: the vagaries of king or mob.

I'm glad I stuck around to sit in jury seat #13. It's made me value what makes America work that is *not* in the headlines. I'm even fine, in theory, about voting "Not guilty!" But reasonableness has limits. Then atavism sets in, and the uncivil me still dreams of those guards giving that scumbag a punch for me.

At the Johnson Hair Salon

"Across from the church and the good coffeehouse, there's a sign, 'Hair Cut,' and it's just beyond that," said the redheaded novelist at our large oak lunch table. She'd gotten a haircut, a good one, her hapless curls now curving gracefully above the shoulder. It made her look younger, perkier, especially with a purple silk scarf draped just right. I couldn't resist a whisper about who cut it and where.

"Look for a large, storefront window with a fake fireplace," she said loud enough to stop the long-haired playwright, in midsentence, about the narrative unreliability of Humbert Humbert in *Lolita*.

"A fake, really?" I asked. With mornings below zero and "warm" days of twenty degrees, why a fake fire? In Georgia maybe, but this was northern Vermont.

I was at a retreat where thirty writers and artists gathered for three great meals and conversation in between long stints in their individual studios. I liked the communal counterweight to solitude and being with people whose eyes didn't glaze over when the subject was the craft of writing. Nevertheless, over the rhubarb crisp, I drifted away into thoughts of how hair defines us—until I heard: "Americans are stupid!" Somehow, the conversation had shifted from *Lolita* to rednecks who hated gun laws and big government.

"They keep voting against self-interest. It's a mystery," said a wispy-haired poet from San Francisco.

"They don't get it!" said the sculptor who made giant clay sunflowers.

"America is so behind the civilized world when it comes to violence!" said the British poet with clipped certainty, his mustache tinged from a little rhubarb. There were nods, mine included, even as I pictured the London square that, according to the guidebook, until 1867 had Saturday "entertainment" of watching prisoners drawn and quartered by horses running in different directions. I considered mentioning it, but it was time to go.

I had one writing week left and planned, that afternoon, to finish an essay about a childhood memory I got all wrong; but my gray roots were getting to me. I couldn't feel old and write young, so I headed for the main street that was two blocks long and the hair salon with the faux brick fireplace.

The space was big enough for a dozen fancy sinks and mirrored walls, but there were only two small sinks, two narrow mirrors, and three people. One was a gray-bearded Vermonter, his head tilted back over the sink, while a sturdy brunette in her midforties bent over him with a water spray. A blonde with black roots, also in her forties, was seated at the large, metal desk, writing in a black notebook.

"Could you, by any chance, do my color?" I'd brought my hair history so she could reproduce my shade of auburn, always tricky. "Sure, sit there," she said, cheerful and definite, as if she needed nothing more. She pointed to the empty chair. "I'll be right over."

The three were talking about a kid who'd been beaten up at the college the other night. "It was so bad, he's still in the hospital," said the guy, rising up from the rinse water.

I'd walked up to the college the day before, a mile uphill on an empty road. It was picture-postcard New England on a winter day, the sun warming the frozen fields, the ice-bent trees, and me. *You can hear yourself think in such quiet*, I thought, keeping a steady pace. The road dead-ended at a redbrick campus with a white New England tower that conveyed historic charm. (Later I found out this campus is fairly new, built on the ruins of an old elementary school). College kids in bright ski hats and funky boots hurried across the quadrangle looking wholesome and safe, as if this were a time warp into the 1950s.

"Can you believe that kid on the motorcycle?" said the brunette. "He's the one who hit the woman and dragged her for five minutes until she was dead. He's now home with his folks." She took out her blow dryer. "While that other kid in Rutland who did about the same thing got jail without bail."

"I think that it was the rapist from the factory that went free," said the no-nonsense blonde at the desk.

The stories were coming so fast, I couldn't keep track—with no mention of Friday night Bingo, or the postman's rheumatism, or someone's baby shower. I'd expected *Our Town,* and this was *Blackboard Jungle* in the heart of pristine America. Upscale Stowe was fifteen miles one way; Smuggler's Notch ski slopes, twenty miles in the other. And in between were dense forests climbing mountain slopes, rolling pastures with cows, and small, scattered towns, some with strip malls, most with freshly painted, old white-clapboard Colonial churches.

Since I'd arrived, my main safety concern was slipping on the ice, especially at 5 a.m. when I headed to my studio before breakfast. It was a three-minute walk from bed to perfect writing space: desk, chair, bookcase, window, period. No "To Do" lists, no family photos, no requests for this or that. For distraction, I'd glance out my window at the river pushing its way between ice and boulders, and most days the words flowed with an imaginative clarity that I didn't have at home.

I, a born New Yorker, hadn't thought about the unlit, deserted streets up here, unless a pickup truck came up fast, skidding around the bend. The more ice, the more fun for those bored with straightaways, but that happened everywhere. What absorbed me up here was the shifting river ice, the rush of water bursting through; and if

I timed it right, I could be on the bridge when gray turned silver in the first light.

"So there's real crime here?" I asked the sturdy brunette who was fastening a towel around my neck. The blonde with black roots came over to answer; she was the more take-charge of the two. "Are you kidding? This is Pill Junction, USA! And I mean pills, not just any drug—OxyContin, Percodan, Demerol. Everyone is on them except us!" They looked calm, but not too calm. She held a color chart to my hair. "I bet the reps from the drug companies take doctors around here out for champagne and caviar three days a week."

"That's how my brother-in-law got hooked," said the sturdy brunette as she tried taming the gruff guy's wild mop.

"The damn government subsidizes the rest," he said, sitting straight up and looking like Falstaff in a red-checkered shirt. "Three kids I know live in a halfway house and get free drugs to fight the drugs!" He shook his head. "Damnedest thing!"

"People around here are poor," the take-charge blonde said, mixing two tubes of my color into a pink bowl. They all faced me, as if this were a trial. "On the street, those big pills can cost eighty bucks, so even with a job, they got a problem. That's why there are so many burglaries."

"Yeah, they take the stuff away from their pets. Dogs, cats, you name it," Falstaff said. He was gruff and pissed off.

"Really? From a vet? How does that work?" I was into it now. The coloring paste in the bowl was redder than I remembered, but hey, I thought, if my hair came out crappy, I still heard this conversation about lives I couldn't invent at my desk or hear in the dining room across the bridge. That Brit who thinks Americans are stupid should get his mustache clipped here. I shouldn't have nodded so easily to his certainty, just because everyone else did.

I'd read about the rising small-town drug use and studies connecting it to the frustrations of white, working-class America. But it felt abstract, far removed, until I sat in this room with two sinks and a reality I had missed on silent walks and in my studio.

"Animals use the same drugs. You just got different doses," said the brunette. "So they go from vet to vet."

"And then they steal more or go on welfare—or both," said my blonde, the red paste now covering half my scalp, her brush strokes speeding up, coming harder, faster.

"Ever see those welfare types in the supermarket?" said Falstaff, standing up. "They stock up on soda, gallons of it, and Twinkies. You know the State even gives them money for lottery tickets?" I almost said *Come on!* but he was bigger than I thought. Six-foot-three at least, with a beer belly pressing against his silver belt buckle.

"That's Vermont for you. Dumber than dumb!" said my blonde, done with me now, and sweeping the floor. She went on a rant about the whole justice system. "The police wouldn't catch a criminal unless he knocked on their door. And those courts, my God! They let every- one off the hook. But not *my* guy."

My scalp was stinging, but I decided against complaining. Her blood was up. "I'm in the courtroom every time he is." Her "guy" was the one who'd robbed her house. She lived out in the woods and her husband, a contractor and a deer hunter, had a wall of guns, plus cameras mounted on trees to track the deer. One of them picked up the kid who broke in, and it was someone she knew. "What a dope!" she said. "He knew I didn't fool around. He should have gone to another house!" It had been two years now, he was out on probation, but never showed up in court. "So now he's looking at eight to ten years. And I'm going to be there when he's sentenced." That got her back in a good mood.

At our roundtable meals, these were the American rednecks, all right: the unfeeling ones who loved guns, killed innocent animals and hated the interfering government. But in this courtroom of hair, they made total sense. My take-charge blonde didn't hate this country kid, just his stupidity. I couldn't argue with that even if I wanted to, which I didn't with stinging color on my scalp. I wasn't afraid; this woman was tough, but not hostile to the drop-ins, like me, who came through the door in this almost all-white town of three thousand—not counting the writers and artists on retreat, the mill workers in a factory down the road, and the college kids up the hill.

In walked one of the college kids, or so I thought. He was a hefty boy with curly hair, a round angelic face, and "Hero" written across his T-shirt. He needed a haircut, said he was from Boston, visiting a friend at the college. The brunette sat him down where Falstaff had been. Falstaff, hands in his jeans pockets, was standing at the desk, not in much of a hurry to pay and leave.

The boy's fingers tapped the air. He was hyper, he said, but settled down as his brunette ran her fingers through his hair, getting a feel for its twists and turns. "So what's going on?" she said, a question no one had asked me. *Was I pegged as the nosy city woman from that lefty retreat?* Within minutes we knew that Hero needed to feel good about himself, went to a shrink three times a week at home, had bad luck with girls and was studying psychology.

"So what have you learned about yourself?" the brunette asked, her voice dropping lower, drawing him out.

"That I am the child of addicts, so I have an addictive personality." She tipped his head back to the sink.

"So what are you addicted to?"

"My dad did cocaine . . . Don't cut too much off, please?" he said, a bit nervous. The scissors begin snipping. "My mom was a wino."

"My dad drank too," my take-charge blonde assured him.

"At least you knew your dad!" the boy said, tapping the chair arm now. "Don't cut too much, please. I only have five bucks."

"Yeah, I did. He died last year, only sixty-five years old." She leaned me back, my head in the sink, the excess color washing away to leave me, I hoped, with a look I could live with. She left for a minute, heading toward the desk.

Falstaff, his wallet out now, asked, "Didn't he die last Christmas Day?"

"Yeah, and Granddaddy died on Christmas Eve three years before that. I've started to really watch out in December."

"Well, you take care," he said, and paused. "I'll get back here before next December."

I waited for his grin, a joke, funny. But no one chuckled, so I held mine in. She gave him change, and I thought this is a special afternoon.

My hair turned out darker than usual, but not bad, a kind of auburn brown that surprised me in the mirror beyond the cash register. I gave a double tip with relief that the old me was there and recognizable, as was a new look created by people to whom I needed to pay attention.

"I didn't know my dad," said Hero. "He died in jail when I was nine. That's why I have low self-esteem." I started to put on my coat and scarf. "Please stop now!" Hero sounded urgent. "I don't have enough for a tip." He said it five more times. He was definitely on something as the hairdresser snipped and blow-dried as if he had a hundred bucks.

Echo across the Road

I like the way small decencies bump against the larger narratives of history, challenging certainties. So of course I like Aron's story of Salach: how he kept coming to milk the "Jewish" cows during the Six Day War in Israel in 1967. All morning the Arab radio stations had been calling for Arabs to rise up and kill the Zionist infidels, so the Jews in this village of three hundred were surprised to see Salach riding his bicycle up the dirt path as usual. "How come you are here?" they asked this Israeli Arab who had crossed the paved road from his Arab village to theirs. "The cows don't know there's a war on!" said Salach, and began cleaning udders and pulling teats as he had for fifteen years.

"We worked in the milk barns together for five years," Aron says, as we drink cappuccinos in Edgar's Café in Manhattan. "Forty years later, we are still in touch. When I visit my mother, I visit Salach." Aron came to the States in the late 1960s after his army service in Israel, met his wife here and stayed. Still, it matters to him that Salach invited him to the weddings of his sons, that his daughters correspond with Salach's daughter, and that the morning after 9/11, "Salach was the first person from Israel to call to see if I was okay, and it was his first call overseas, ever."

"I'd like to meet Salach," I say, wondering what keeps their friendship intact despite the ongoing Arab-Israeli crises. I hadn't expected Salach's loyalty, even if he did live in Israel proper—within the original UN borders established in 1948.

"No problem," says Aron, and two days later it is all arranged. Next month when I'm in Israel, I am invited to meet Salach, in his home, in his village.

Six kilometers north of Akko or Acco or Acre (the name depending on whether Muslims, Crusaders, Turks, British, or Israelis controlled this fortress city north of Haifa), you'll find Aron's village on the left, Salach's village on the right. Both have long entrance roads lined with palm trees. The Jewish village is flat, laid out on a grid of a dozen streets close to the Mediterranean shoreline; the Arab village is tucked into a hillside rising just high enough to see the waves hitting the rocky coast.

I turn left first: to the community I've been to many times to visit my Aunt Hilde who, in 1937, fled my father's German village with twenty-nine families that came here as a group. So while I grew up in Queens, New York, my father's Benheim neighbors started again on 600 dunams (148 acres) of land, bought from a Turkish prince with gambling debts. There were no cow barns and green fields then; only sand, dirt, and British soldiers with guns who said, on that first day, that the Jews could stay *if* they could build a watchtower, bunkers, and a barbed-wire fence before nightfall. Otherwise, bill of sale or no, they had to leave. Much to the soldiers' surprise, the group finished in time, driven by fear and great hope. As Jacob, a second cousin of my father's, wrote in the village archival history: "Everyone knew we had escaped hell . . . and so even in this barren spot, people felt a measure of control over their lives. In Germany, everything had been taken away: our swords, our guns, our civil rights. Here at least we could defend ourselves."

Aron was born in one of the thirty, small, concrete houses that the pioneers built with red shingle roofs reminiscent of the life left behind. Inside, the same Schwarzwald cuckoo clocks chimed in tiny rooms with dark, German armoires and lace doilies spread out on every tabletop. Other immigrants have since settled in the village—Jews fleeing Iraq and Iran and Syria—but I knew only those who made *Linzertorte* and *Maultaschen* dumplings floating in beef broth. They were the *Yekkas*, as Israelis call German Jews, the ones who remembered planting every carob and almond tree lining their streets. And pointed out the watchtower with the menorah on top; it was where Aron's mother once stood guard to warn against Arab attacks. And took me to the Memorial Room, built to honor the 126 deported from Benheim by the Nazis and murdered in Auschwitz, Theresienstadt, and Riga. Every name was carved into a wall of stone lit by an eternal flame, and mounted beside them was a Torah rescued from the old synagogue on *Kristallnacht* by their Christian neighbors: "*Ja*, Nazi orders or no, they saved it for us, and so we have it still!" A small decency amid so much horror, but a story these villagers needed to tell: like Salach coming to milk the cows

❖

To get to Salach's house, my friend from Haifa drives me through the all-Arab town, winding through quaint streets, past market stalls selling everything from hummus to lutes to *kaffiyeh* scarves. I expected the timelessness of this *souk*, but not the Internet café on the corner or the bright blue sign in Hebrew with a phoenix. "It's for an Israeli insurance company," my friend Israel says.

Yes, that is his name, not a metaphor. Or rather the name he adopted when he arrived in 1944 on a *Kindertransport* from Romania. He was fourteen. "I used to be called Vasile," he tells me, "which in my synagogue was Yisrael. So the switch felt right." I think so too, for this man I've long admired as representing the best of this country: tough, empathetic, innovative—someone who, like so many others, managed to shake off the yoke of Europe's anti-Semitism and reinvent himself in this new nation. At seventeen, he joined the Haganah to fight for Israel's right to exist; at forty, he became a professor of engineering at the Technion in Haifa; and at sixty-eight, he started a small tech company. On this day, he is my interpreter, translating Hebrew, which Salach speaks fluently, into English for me.

We head up the hill, as instructed, and near the top is Salach's large, white villa trimmed in blue, "a good luck color for the Arabs," says Israel. Good luck, yes, but also great perseverance, according to my Aunt Hilde, who knows Salach well. "Here is a man with no education, whose grandfather was a serf and who, through hard work, has built a mansion!" she'd told me over lunch. "If every Arab was like Salach, we'd all be living in peace."

Salach's daughter Dalal, a delightful woman whom I met the day before—she's an administrator in the office of the Jewish village—is waving from the courtyard. She is dressed in black pants and black top, her head full of black curls, very Western and stylish. There are three other women peering at us from the kitchen, all in headscarves, but without veils. "They probably won't come out," Israel whispers. "Women traditionally don't take part in such things." Dalal is less traditional not only in dress. There is an independence in her step that signals comfort with herself and with strangers. Her smile makes that comfort reciprocal.

Dalal leads us into a large, airy living room with several gray print couches, matching chairs, and a big Toshiba TV. I could be in Tel Aviv, except for a brass-hammered page from the Qur'an on one wall and a framed poster of a crowd facing a minaret under a banner of Arabic writing. "It is the pilgrimage to Mecca," Dalal says. "My father has made hajj four times since 1990."[1] She sounds very proud, which surprises me, given her secular attire. I expected religion to

---

1 Going to Mecca is not easy to do with an Israeli passport, my friend Israel tells me later. His Arab contractor also made hajj, but only after great difficulty getting a visa.

be either/or, but then I also expected dark burkas everywhere in this village.

What makes the mix of modernity and Islam seem natural is the abundance of family photos, past and present. Snapshots of newborn twins are tucked into the frame of the pilgrimage to Mecca. Several midsize photos flank the right of the Qur'an, and on the left is a large, framed portrait of a sturdy man in a white cap and white mustache and Dalal's smile. It must be Salach, looking very much the patriarch. Crammed into his frame are a dozen photos of children and grand-children. "That was taken on my father's 70th birthday last year," says Dalal and takes out a blue album to show us more handsome faces celebrating, the young stylishly bare-headed like Dalal; the elders wearing traditional caps and headscarves.

"Look over there," says Dalal, pointing to a woman's portrait near the TV. "She lived until ninety-nine—under the Turks, the British, and now the Israelis." Dalal keeps talking, and Israel looks pleased, especially when Dalal says the Israelis are the best to live under. "She likes our social services, the pensions, and health care. She doesn't have to worry," he says. Later, back in Haifa, when we tell Israel's wife this story, she says, "But of course Arabs will say that! You are naïve. What else would they say to us directly?" Israel and I couldn't argue with that, but I kept thinking *She didn't see Dalal's confident bounce without deception. Besides, Dalal could have said nothing at all.*

Salach appears, true to his photo in his white hat and mustache. Dalal takes his arm. "This is my father." He bows slightly. "And this is Mrs. Schwartz, the friend of Aron . . ." I bow slightly, not sure whether a handshake is better. "And this is her friend who will translate for us." Israel smiles. Salach nods.

Dalal tells us how her father retired four years ago from working in dairy barns. "They begged him to come back to supervise, at least part time, and so he went two hours a day. But I insisted to drive him, no more bike riding. After this birthday, we told him it's inconceivable to work after seventy. People would think he was in need despite children to care for him. It would be a disgrace. It couldn't be." Dalal sounds neither bossy nor obsequious, and Salach seems amused. There is no sign of feeling threatened by a young person, a daughter no less, telling his story for him. This is a confident man.

"I just retired too," says Israel, "and I also had my seventieth birthday." Salach congratulates him, and they start talking with many nods and sighs about the subject of shared wistfulness: retirement. Salach says he goes at four every morning to the mosque, comes home and sleeps until ten, goes to the mosque again, and then sits over coffee with other men his age. He misses the old days, working at full steam. Israel nods, saying he stays busy with some technical projects, but one of his children now runs the day-to-day operation of his company. More nods.

How glad I am that Israel has come! He's managed, within ten minutes, to turn "Jew" and "Arab," the labels for those living a political chasm apart, into two amicable men of seventy, just talking. Children. Retirement. Common ground.

"I built this with my own hands," Salach says, waving his arm as if in a blessing for the three wings of his house. What began in 1951 as a single room for his wife, mother, and one child now has enough space to accommodate eight children and twenty-seven grandchildren, who either live here or visit regularly from nearby Akko or Nahariya. One son is a *sharia* judge; another, a doctor; a third is in construction; a fourth runs the garage of trucks and huge tractors in Aron's village; and Dalal, the only unmarried daughter, works in the office over there.

I am surprised by their success in a Jewish state and wonder how typical that is. True, Israeli Arabs are citizens, with representatives in Israel's Parliament, and full rights to social services, health and educational benefits. But they don't serve in the army, and many Jews worry that they could be a fifth column during wartime. Unofficial discrimination exists in jobs and housing "not unlike your minorities in America," Israel tells me after we leave. "And certainly not all Israel's Arabs are prosperous, like Salach." But Israel knows several who have done very well: "My contractor, who started with nothing, owns one of the biggest construction firms in Haifa. Another is a professor. One heads a department in the hospital. One fixes doors, a good business." He then says a variation of what my Aunt Hilde said: "We could live very well with Arabs if not for the stupidity of our leaders on both sides."

Salach's village has grown from one hundred residents in 1947 to three thousand five hundred in 2009—and is still growing. In fact, Aron's village is about to transfer, with government approval, sixty dunams of land to this Arab village, an ironic reversal of what was happening on the West Bank a few kilometers away. "They need the land, and we need the money," my Aunt Hilde told me. The Jewish villagers had invested in a plastics factory that hadn't worked out. Plus, many of their children had moved away as adults although most, unlike Aron in New York, had stayed in Israel.

"I am not from this village," says Salach after we start eating from the platters of dates, grapes, almonds, cashews, and olives, fresh from the orchards outside. Or so I imagine—not at all like my Aunt Hilde's high cholesterol delights across the road. Salach's wife, in a headscarf, has brought the food. She is plump, dignified, and after being introduced, she retreats to a chair in the corner. "My birth village is nearer to Lebanon," Salach continues, "and was destroyed by the Israeli army during the 1947 war. I fled to the hills." I listen for anger, but hear sadness. Israel nods. I know he fought in that war, trying to protect Jewish settlements, and I worry that common ground is slipping out from under us. But the code of civility prevails. Dalal pours us tea, stronger than coffee, and everyone drinks. A guest is a guest in an Arab home.

Salach tells us how "some hotheads" from his boyhood village were recruited by Arab leadership to attack Kibbutz Cabri. The Israelis retaliated. His father was on the roof with a white handkerchief, but they shot him down. Silence. "But I can understand that," Salach says, his voice steady. "It was revenge for a wrong." *Does he mean it?* I wonder. *Would I?* The code of an eye-for-an-eye has ruled these lands forever, the turn-the-other-cheek teachings of Jesus, even as aspiration, never took root. "The Israelis had to do what they had to do," Salach says softly. No one nods now.

Many Jews in this region of Western Galilee have told me that in 1947 "if the Arabs didn't attack us, we left them alone." Evidently Salach's current village did not fight, but a nearby Arab village had a group that fought vigorously, and a bullet killed my Aunt Hilde's friend as she worked in the communal kitchen. That Arab village was destroyed, except for its mosque.

"Many decisions depended on the Israeli commander," Israel tells me at dinner that night. "Most were humane, but some were not." His voice saddens with a memory of those days when he was seventeen and fighting for the first time. "In one unfriendly Arab village, there was an old man who could barely walk. I wanted to help him, but my commander said no. A minute later the side of his head was gone, and he died before me. I still see this image today."

Baruch Ha Shem! Blessed be the Name! Two names for god—Yawah and Allah—now inhabit, for me, the same phrase of gratefulness for surviving with good fortune. *Baruch Ha Shem* is what Solly L., one of two Jews from my father's village to survive the concentration camps, kept saying. A man let him work in the kitchen of the camp, *Baruch Ha Shem*. A friend dropped bread and water into a deep hole in the ground where he was being punished, *Baruch Ha Shem*. Later he met his wonderful wife in the DP camp, *Baruch Ha Shem* and became a kosher butcher in Baltimore, and raised two sons who are rabbis and whose families, twenty-seven children and grandchildren, dominate his living room in photos. Just like Salach's. *Baruch Ha Shem!*

And now Salach keeps saying *Baruch Ha Shem!* in Hebrew: to tell how he survived after the Israelis attacked his birth village, and he fled. They captured him later and took him by truck to the Jordanian border, where he was dropped off. He had no food or money, but another Palestinian with a truck, who was traveling with his family, took him along into Syria. The Syrians didn't want them, and, if not for this man, *Baruch Ha Shem*, he would have been badly beaten or worse. He made his way to Lebanon, hungry and dirty, and *Baruch Ha Shem*, a janitor in a factory took pity on him, fed him soup and let him sleep on the factory floor. He slipped across the border into Israel and eventually made his way to this village. He was picking oranges in the field on the day the Israelis came in a truck and gave out identity cards, which allowed him to stay in Israel. And so, forty days after he was deported, he became a legal resident of the new state and even received a small plot of land. *Baruch Ha Shem*.

My father bought two plots for graves, not far from Aron's house in the village. No one expected it. Here was a man who, after great dislocation, seemed to thrive for thirty-six years in his adopted country, America. Yet, two months before he died, he told my mother that he wanted to be buried in the Jewish homeland. So when his heart stopped suddenly in 1973, my mother—along with my sister, Stu, and me—flew his body across the ocean and watched as men in shorts and blue kibbutz caps lowered his pine coffin into the land of Israel.

True, my father had been a Zionist ever since, as a young soldier in World War I, he saw the hate of German comrades, who liked *him* well enough, for the less-assimilated Polish Jews. He later wrote, "For the first time I realized that what I saw could happen to the Jewish people everywhere, and that impression never disappeared. It was the reason I knew right away in 1933 to leave Hitler's Germany."

This insight explains why he worked tirelessly for Jewish statehood, always raising funds to ensure Jewish survival. And why in the end he decided to lay claim to this ancestral land, which so many claim. Signs of past occupancy were everywhere: the ancient Greek perfume bottle we found in a seawall; the shards of Roman pottery on the beach after a downpour; the insignia of the Knights of Saint John, dug up in my Aunt Hilde's garden; the mosaic floor of an early Christian church, a minute's walk from my father's grave. And down the road: the spot where Jesus healed a sick child. The local Jewish version is that the mother, a Canaanite, asked for help, and Jesus at first answered, "I can only help Jews." But this woman persisted. "You help dogs. Am I not as important as a dog?" And so Jesus cured the child.

Not quite the International Bible version, but a worthy parable of tolerance and faith (Matthew 15:21–28) to pass down for almost two thousand years. Still, the Nazis posted signs all over Germany: No Jews or Dogs Allowed. And three weeks after my father's funeral, Syria and Egypt attacked on Yom Kippur, the highest holy day of the Jews. I remember military planes racing low in the sky as I placed a stone of remembrance on my father's grave in a tiny cemetery of thirty graves. Three decades later, my mother lies beside my father, and I hear more planes, still fast and low, as I search the sandy, red soil for two stones to mark memory before reciting the Kaddish, the prayer for the dead—all of them.

Aron tells me on the phone that he and his eighty-nine-year-old mother went to visit Salach when Aron was in Israel last week. He was surprised by the enthusiasm Salach's wife had for meeting his mother; it was their first time. "His wife is always gracious, but reserved. I didn't think she spoke much Hebrew. But she and my mother sat together, chatting in a corner, and when we were leaving, she gave my mother such enormous hugs! She was clearly happy that she came."

"Why did she do it?" I am thinking of the latest headlines of battles raging, rockets being lobbed over borders, old men dying in the crossfire.

"I don't know. She must really like my mother!" But then Aron remembers something: "I think my mother was telling her how she had to flee her village in Germany and what hardships they went through coming here as refugees. Maybe Salach's wife had sympathy. She could understand because the same had happened to her." I love this story, I say. I love that face-to-face stories can modify the anonymity of hate.

"Yes, maybe that was it," Aron says tentatively.

A few days later, he calls to say he wants to organize a get-together of the two villages. Last year he organized a fiftieth reunion of his village schoolmates and that was a great success. They came from all over Israel, so why not this? "It probably won't be held in either village, not this first time, but in the open fields between us. Maybe a potluck supper, picnic-style! The Jews could bring their food, the gefilte fish, *Maultaschen*, whatever they want. And the Arabs could bring their foods."

"What a great idea!" I meant it. While politicians continue the barrage of rhetoric about death and revenge, Aron is planning the details of a potluck possibility: "First the children could play games of volleyball or soccer, and then we could sit down on lawn chairs and eat together, celebrating our seventy years side-by-side. You know very few of us visit each other's homes, and the two villages have never met together officially. It's time."

FIG. 14. Preparing a Thanksgiving dinner with unwarranted optimism—
Ann Arbor, 1962. Courtesy of author.

1890

ƐⱰƐⱠɎᘰ ᘓᓍⱠⱠƐᘘƐ

—FOR—

YOUNG WOMEN

PRINCETON NEW JERSEY

FIG. 15. Brochure for Evelyn College, 1890, which is "now a two-family house next door." Courtesy of Princeton University Archives.

FIG. 16. The last class of Evelyn College, 1897, which hoped "to be Princeton University's sister school, what Radcliffe was to Harvard." Collection of the Historical Society of Princeton.

FIG. 17. The day the men laid water pipes under the big oak of Evelyn Place—"it died the following spring." Courtesy of author.

FIG. 18. Don and Ruth Moore of Glen Acres, "who owned the same ranch model we did, three houses down—and knew all things house." Courtesy of Maggie Yurachek Photography.

FIG. 19. Glen Acres children playing together, "and everyone wanted to keep it that way." Courtesy of Ted Peck.

FIG. 20. My granddaughter baking *Berches*, a favorite Schwarzwald recipe for bread. Courtesy of author with permission of Carly Mazer.

FIG. 21. *Learning Each Other's Historical Narrative*, written by Israeli and Palestinian history teachers "to tell their double narrative." Courtesy of PRIME (Peace Research Institute in the Middle East) and available at http://vispo.com/prime/leohn1.pdf.

FIG. 22. Salach and Aron, an Israeli Arab and Israeli Jew, friends for sixty years: "Salach's phone call to me in New York City after 9/11 was the first call I received from Israel and his first call, ever, overseas." Courtesy of Aron Berlinger.

FIG. 23. Hugging our way back to health as "we play the hand that's dealt" after a heart attack and breast cancer, two weeks apart. Courtesy of author.

FIG. 24. The OnStage Senior Ensemble, now of McCarter Theatre, rehearsing stories. "'It's called documentary theater,' she said . . . and I, at sixty-five, thought why not?" Courtesy of author.

FIG. 25. Our gang at the lake house, 2009. Courtesy of author.

FIG. 26. My sister-in-law and I on the trail in Croatia, looking for redefinitions. Courtesy of author.

PART 3

Storyscapes

Without knowing the force of words,
it is impossible to know more.

—CONFUCIUS

Story on a Winter Beach

Spirit is the art of making what's
blocked start moving again.

—RUMI, A THIRTEENTH-CENTURY PERSIAN POET

When I was forty-seven and diagnosed with breast cancer, I gathered every good-luck story I could: about my college roommate's mother who had breast cancer thirty-five years before; about my colleague who called to say she'd had a double mastectomy twelve years earlier; about my good friend Sue who had had three cancerous lymph nodes and ten months of chemotherapy and looked terrific three years later, better than before.

These stories helped me get on with my life as mother, wife, teacher, writer, daughter, and friend. The darker stories of those having problems, of those who didn't make it, felt dangerous, like a jinx. So I stayed away from the breast cancer support groups and avoided articles with titles like "The Anguish of Breast Cancer" and "Victims of Mastectomy." I wanted no anguish, no victimhood—only lucky stories that encouraged me, six weeks after my mastectomy, to say "I *had* breast cancer."

Years later, I still say "had." But the further I got from my mastectomy, the more I realized that my old definition of "good" story, i.e., cancer free, was too limited. It allowed luck to override the power of spirit; and stories of spirit, unconcerned with luck, are the *really* good stories.

I first realized that on the beach of Cape May, walking in mid-January with poet Judy Rowe Michaels. It was maybe two years after my mastectomy, and we were both teaching in the Cape May Writers' Getaway, held every year over the Martin Luther King weekend to lift the winter spirits. The crisp air and frozen sand let us move at a good clip, and I marveled at her energy after a second round of chemotherapy. Yes, it made her sick for a day or two, yes, she had lost her hair, "but I'm fine!" she said and started telling me about the house she'd just bought, her first. It sat on a ridge of New Jersey's Sourland Mountains northwest of me: a renovated hunting cabin with big windows, a wood-burning stove, and—best yet—a hot tub in a garden off the back porch. So much better, she said, than the cramped second floor she and her husband had rented in nearby Hopewell for years: "A health-giving space, something we always wanted, but never got around to buying until now."

Maybe she'd live in it a year, maybe twenty years, maybe a few months. It didn't seem to matter, which is what I loved. She never mentioned luck. She had made her own by buying a mountain house and going daily into its "big bedroom/study with its big view." And all the anger and fear we feel when we might die went into new poems like "No Guarantees," which moved beyond those dark feelings into a life she savored—whatever lay ahead:

> I drink fresh coffee my husband brings in
> from the café where I used to write at dawn,
> I drink fragrance of white stock and tulips,
> the bright, pointy, yellow ones traced in green.
> I have washed, combed my dying hairs,
> welcomed the nurse changing sheets,
> over which the doctors stand disputing.

I count invisible morning stars to find
new statistics, number off flower petals,
I imagine I taste a new drug in the coffee that no one
will yet guarantee, like a moon pit where you might
fall forever or crawl up the other side, gleaming.
We trim the tulips' stems to make them
live a little longer; the coffee's
gone cold. X rays are shadows that grow
in the long afternoons, and where they lead, you follow
into an uncertain twilight, trailing your IV.

I told Judy's story to another writer friend, Barbara D., who had chemotherapy that fall. "Two years and Judy's still in the house," I said, as we walked the beach—again at Cape May—that was soft this year from the warm winter, our feet sinking with each step. Barbara smiled, and I told her that I liked her wig. It gave her a zippy look, a thick, blond, Buster Brown cut, much more dramatic than her fine, wavy chestnut. We talked about needing good stories to survive, and she said the story she most counted on was her own. She'd repeat it whenever she could: how she'd fainted in class, how her students had called 911, how the ER doctors had seen a shadow that meant more than a bad reaction to antibiotics, and, most important, how her skill in storytelling ("I got more precise, and dramatic, with each retelling") helped to save her. Doctors, nurses, orderlies, and nurses' aides all paid closer attention. She'd gotten better care, she was sure— not to mention a sense of control. "Now I feel fine!" she said, leaving cancer behind her. We talked about the power of the verb "had" vs. "has"—and how cancer as past tense makes the future more real. She told me about a friend of hers with breast cancer who had just gotten married without waiting for the pathology report. *Why should she wait?* we both agreed in delight.

I told her of my husband's mantra after our double whammy: "You have to play the hand you are dealt, and play it as well as you can."

He'd had a heart attack four days after the doctor discovered my lump and had his angioplasty three days before my mastectomy. We were not yet fifty, and the thought that we could die so early had never crossed our minds. But there it was, our safe world unhinged. So now what? I embraced Stu's mantra, his positivism, and him—and felt less afraid, more hopeful.

Which is probably why, ten days after a mastectomy, I decided to hold a Passover seder. Nothing big: just for Stu, our children, and me. I wasn't religious, didn't even like ritual, but somehow I needed to eat the traditional dishes and sing half-remembered melodies from seders of my childhood, always led by Uncle Julius, always ending with singing about a hapless goat, bought and eaten: *Had Gadya, Had Gadya.*

I published an essay, "A Night for Haroset"—about this night of celebration, wanting whoever was up there to be impressed "and see us as solid types, not flaky," agreeing "that we should be around a lot longer, cancer and heart attack notwithstanding." I acknowledged my "Why me?" rage, which intensified every time I had to read aloud, "Thank you, God," again and again. As others praised freedom and escape from Egypt with "May the Merciful One be blessed in heavens and on earth!" I sat silent, thinking: *What about the Holocaust? And the children of Somalia? And Mai Lai? And what about me, us? We're good people . . .*

I didn't dwell on the despair of looking in the bathroom mirror at my jagged scar. I moved to the pleasures of an evening as sweet as the honeyed apples I had chopped despite my stitches, buoyed by a continuity beyond our own lives. Passover, itself a bittersweet celebration of survival, made me part of a long story that gave me new spirit, and I wrote: "Even if the cancer spreads, and Stu slumps to the floor tomorrow, we are saying words that have been handed down for three thousand years, and they will be repeated next year, no matter what." I held onto that comfort.

A year or two later I received a note about this essay—from Judy Michaels. She'd read it in *Calyx* and had been comforted by it. She passed it on:

I sent copies off right away to three women friends—two Jewish, one not—all of whom have struggled with frightening health crises in their families. One, my office mate, came over to hug me the day she read it and said, "You always know what I need."

Reading her letter, I realized I'd become as brave as Judy, who had bought the mountain house, and Barbara's friend, who'd gotten married before reading her pathology report. My story had come full circle, a gift with the power to uplift. No matter that I hadn't felt particularly brave that night and had wept on many others, I had captured a good three hours, and it had turned my small steps of risk into full strides of bravery that others joined, as we carried each other along, lucky or not.

Go Away, Bear

The night before I leave for ten days in the Canadian Rockies, a friend comes by with three tiny bells, jingling softly. "They are bear bells," he says, "to warn bears away and keep you safe." I tie them to my daypack, thinking bears must have great hearing, but feel protected. Until our guide, Jos, asks on day one, "What's that noise?" I point to my bells, and Jos laughs. "Oh that's what we find in bear scat, especially grizzly scat!" I keep the bells on anyway; they weigh nothing.

It's early September, and I'm hiking in Banff, Yoho, and Kootenay National Parks with my friends Tod, Linda, and Gail. We are on a Backroads trip that combines a week of challenging day hikes with hotel nights on soft pillows. Stu and I had gone to Provence with Backroads and loved it, but after arrhythmia twice on the steep hills, he had decided no more hiking trips.

There are twelve of us who have gathered in the town of Banff, including a young couple from Idaho who say they've done the Iron-man twice.

"What's that?" I ask. We're in the van driving to our first trailhead.

"You swim 2.4 miles, bike for 112 miles, and run for 26.2 miles," says the guy, an ER doctor. I'm glad about the doctor part.

"Great! You do this in how many days?" I ask, impressed.

"It has to be in under seventeen hours," says his lawyer wife, gorgeous and matter-of-fact. "Or else it doesn't count."

I'd been worrying about my sciatica, how it would fare on a five- or six-hour hike on steep terrain. Now I'm thinking abandonment—*She was too old and slow*—until a forty-something woman complains of two bad knees, ruined by playing college basketball for UCLA. She's big. I will stick with her, plus my three friends. We're the oldest in this group, all on Medicare, and with an assortment of aches—a half-frozen shoulder, a pulled calf muscle, sciatica—but we still play first-rate tennis three times a week (on good Advil days).

Our group has come for the challenge and beauty of spectacular mountains, lakes, and waterfalls, the best anywhere we've been told; but also, though no one mentions this allure, for the bears. To touch wildness, feel alive with risk *and* live to tell the tale, that's the gestalt of this world that you won't find, say, in the civilized charms of Provence.

Bears are in everyone's stories, as we walk up the trail in twos and threes, close enough to hear each other. A woman from Chicago says she thought she saw a black bear yesterday at twilight near where a dozen cars had stopped on the highway shoulder. A guy from Pennsylvania says he was two hundred yards upstream from a grizzly once, when fly fishing in Oregon: "Fortunately, there were plenty of salmon for him to eat!" He chuckles. We chuckle. I tell of the grizzly that came into a friend's tent in Alaska after she accidently camped on a bear "superhighway." "Go away, bear!" she said, trying not to sound too aggressive or too meek. "And it went away!"

"Go away, bear!" we joke all morning—and while sitting on boulders, eating lunch beside Yoho Lake with its unbelievable clear water in three shades of green. "Yoho" is an expression of wonder and awe by First Nations people and a perfect name for this wild spot, three hours from a paved road. Not far from us, overnighters have strung their food high on a pole. "So the bears can't reach it," says Jos, our guide, but assures us that bears avoid humans "and you are a noisy group!" So we eat our turkey sandwiches, berries, nuts, and dried fruit with only a glance into the forest.

We walk the ridge and then head towards a dot of sea green visible through the trees: Emerald Lake, our destination for that night. "Go away, bear!" is still heard with giggles until we reach a steep, treeless moraine. "Avalanche country," says Jos. We look up at precarious boulders and down as small rocks roll under our feet, and within ten minutes two people fall. No more bear jokes; we concentrate on every step.

Late in the day, on the last mile of flat trail that hugs Emerald Lake, we meet a woman in shorts and a tank top heading up the trail we've come down. She takes out her earbuds and asks, "Which way to the high lake?" We, with our daypacks, rain gear, trail mix, double water bottles, and walking poles, are speechless. She has no water or daypack; she's alone and thinks she can climb the moraine and cross the alluvial fan of rushing streams that sometimes have logs as bridges, though you can't count on them after a heavy rain. Jos, with her savvy and good cheer, says: "Yoho Lake is hours away, and it's getting dark . . ." The woman nods, reinserts her earbuds and keeps walking. Jos shakes her head. "That's why we had forty rescues in this park last year. People think they are walking to the mall."

There's a "Bears and People" pamphlet at the ranger station. We laugh at the main advice, "AVOID an encounter," but study its tips: make noise; watch for bear signs, such as droppings and torn-up logs; stay in groups. If you see one, stand tall, don't run and form a huddle to look big. Four hikers are the minimum number for safety. Comforting, until we hear that a bear cub in Yellowstone National Park recently ran between four hikers and the angry mama charged. One person lost an arm; another is on the critical list. I touch my bear bells. Doing everything right doesn't help if your luck turns bad.

Ours stays with us. We have blue skies, no bugs, and every hike has its own surprise. One day it is charred logs, like black pick-up sticks, strewn for miles from a forest fire that burned 13 percent of Kootenay National Park. It was ten years ago, but things grow so slowly up here that the new spruce and pine are only two feet high. The next day it is a steep stone staircase carved into the mountain. You don't look down, no point. Someone goes before you, someone is waiting behind you, and you just go. The day after it is fifteen minutes on a very narrow ledge in Banff National Park, trying to reach the Plain of Six Glaciers Teahouse. We hold the safety wire and look up for mountain goats that are said to graze high above us.

No thoughts of sciatica by the time I cross the wide, rushing stream with stepping-stones that disappear in a heavy downpour, the one time I use my rain gear in eight days. What I feel is delightfully brave with that special rush of optimism and denial: someone before, someone after, go. That's all there is.

I begin to sign postcards with "Love, the Mountain Woman," imbued with the spirit of Mary Schaffer, a Grace Kelly type from mainline Philadelphia who was transformed by this world. She came to the Canadian Rockies in 1889 with her husband, a botanist recording plant life, especially wildflowers. Her wonderful drawings hang in the Whyte Museum in Banff along with photos of her. My favorite photo is when Schaffer sheds her long, high-collared dresses for a fringed buckskin jacket. She is life size, as she sits in a tent, binoculars pointed to the high peaks. Schaffer went back to Philadelphia with her husband, but when he died suddenly, she returned to live permanently as artist and adventurer in this raw and dangerous beauty.

Our hike to Helen Lake is canceled because an aggressive grizzly bear is spotted in the area. Park policy is to move the people, not the animals, whenever possible, so we are to hike ten miles away. "Don't worry!" Jos assures us. "You are 374 times more likely to die from lightning than from a bear attack." I'm reassured until someone says there is far more lightning than bears. Later, on a website called the Grizzly Bear Blog, I find more feel-good facts:

1 person out of 16,000 commits murder but only 1 grizzly bear out of 50,000 ever kills someone and only 1 black bear out of one million does. So people are much more dangerous than bears!

As far as bear danger in general (same website): You are twelve times more likely to die of a bee sting, ten times more likely to die of a dog attack, thirteen times from snakes, seventeen from spiders, and one hundred fifty from tornadoes.

Jos carries bear spray (really pepper spray) on her hip, next to her walkie-talkie, but has never used it in ten years of leading Backroad trips. She did use it once, near her house not far from Banff, at night. A grizzly fake-charged her twice, and she was sure it would charge again for real. When it did, she sprayed, and the bear retreated. "You have to know which way the wind is blowing," she laughs, "or you spray yourself." We like this story in which competence reigns. Jos, I should add, trains a survival unit of the British Army, so spraying a bear that is three feet away is part of her everyday cool.

On our next-to-last hiking day, Tod, Linda, Gail, and I decide to hike on our own, only half a day, so we can spend time in the hotel's Jacuzzi. This is vacation after all, and we are at Lake Louise, population one thousand, which is civilization around here. The Canadian Pacific Railroad wanted wealthy train travelers to visit in the late nineteenth century, so it built grand hotels in Banff (in 1888) and at Lake Louise (in 1890), where hordes of travelers, rich and middle class, now come for gorgeous views as they sip a cappuccino or martini. Hiking is optional.

We ask the clerk at the hotel desk for a trail map, and he hands me bear spray. "Really?" I ask. "Around here?"

"Just a precaution," he assures us and points out where to pull and press. I put the canister where I usually keep one of two water bottles and tell Tod: "I'll carry it, but you'll have to use it!" He is a sailor, so at least he knows which way the wind is blowing.

We hike upwards, passing a young woman jogging, a man with two leashed dogs, and a father carrying a toddler as if this were anywhere. The Bow River rushes beside us, the woods thin out and thicken again, trails crisscross, twigs break. We spot a squirrel, a fox, three lovely magpies, and the last of the wildflowers, called western anemone or "hippie on a stick," because of its gray hair blowing. We see a "Beware Bear" poster and keep walking, as if life were no more dangerous than on Broadway at night. We feel like Lewis and Clark, conquering the wild as our shadows lengthen, the light dims, the bells get louder—and we look for the intersecting trail of return.

Writing with Carly

This poem is on our refrigerator door:

> I love you, to the moon and stars and all the
> Way up to the planet mars.
> So one day if I fly up there
> You'll know I love you anywhere.

It has a smiley face above it and "I love you!" in a heart below it—
and was written by our granddaughter Carly in the days when she
felt like a writer. The feeling began at age four when she read at a
family gathering, "On Chanukah you wear a yarmulke!" Everyone
clapped, laughed and hugged her. You're a poet, we said—and I
remembered how, at her age, I'd read my poems at family gather-
ings and beamed.

I bought Carly a writing journal, and she filled it with stories and
poems, most often composed while looking out her bedroom window
at falling leaves, snowflakes, and spring blossoms. The spelling was
her own, but no matter. She proudly read her stories about strawberry
dreams and rainbows and a daisy trying to grow in a field of daffodils
(my favorite).

By second grade, the spelling was correct, thanks to nightly drills
requiring original sentences for all thirty words of the week. In third

grade, after a poetry unit in school, she told me her poem on my fridge was not good. The first line was "way too long" and "mars" needed a capital. But I love it! I said, especially the last two lines that made love fly everywhere. She shrugged. What did *I* know about rhyme and rhythm?

Fourth grade included a researched report on Northern New Jersey, complete with hand-made maps and photos based on a field trip, plus a "book" of stories based on paintings of Picasso, Renoir, Monet, and Van Gogh. Good assignments from a conscientious, enthusiastic teacher, but they took up free time and involved deadlines and grades. "Writing is hard!" Carly started to say.

I told her how my last book took twelve years to finish, and soon after that, she asked, "Can we write something together?" I was thrilled and told her how a friend and her daughter chose a topic to write about each month using email. She liked the idea, and I pictured a lively exchange of poems and stories of our inside and outside lives.

Our plan was for me to think up three topics, and Carly would choose the one we'd write on, a new one each month. The first month was "Purple," and I wrote six versions of the same poem, worrying. I had taught college writing for thirty years and knew how to help writers find their words, but this was my granddaughter. I hadn't a clue. Should I write as I usually did? For honesty—and to see what comes out? Or should I write for a nine-year-old: something simple, suitable, and inspirational? I decided to try for both. "Who should send first?" I asked in an email around week three when I hadn't heard. "You," she answered, and so I sent this poem, purposely making my first line "way too long":

PURPLE IS THE BEST

Pink was not for me, a girl who loved horses more than dolls.
Yellow was too weak, like a pale sun.
White, too much responsibility,
Red and Orange, way too showy.
Black, scary.

I wanted Blue of a bold sky,
Rust to match my freckles,
And go-everywhere Beige.
But lately, it's Purple I love best,
The color of promise in sunsets
And what you find when you stare
Into burning logs
Long enough.

A day later she sent this:

PURPLE IS . . .
Purple is a juicy grape
waiting on a vine,
Purple is the sky
before the sun begins to shine.
Purple is the bottom
of exquisite rainbows.
Purple is a color
that always seems to glow.

I loved how we'd just had a conversation in purple, and I imagined great things. I'd invite all my writer friends with grandchildren to follow our plan, and we'd soon have a new kind of writing movement, across generations. There would be no grades, no rules, just one voice encouraging another to speak.

Dear Carly,

I love your poem . . . and it's great that we both see the glow in purple. I'm putting yours on the refrigerator door.

Love,
Grandma Mim

I wanted to praise, but not overpraise, always remembering the guy in a writing class I once joined in Greenwich Village. He came with the first three pages of a promising story, and everyone said, "Keep going! It's great!" (This from a group not generous with praise.) The same thing happened for three more weeks—he'd bring a beginning, we'd love it—and then he disappeared for good. His talent scared him, and our enthusiasm scared him more. Like the feeling I can have after writing something I like, sure that it will never happen again.

For our next topic, Carly suggested an animal. If I named four of them, she'd pick one. I emailed "Turtle, Oyster, Lion, or Hummingbird" and got back "HUMMINGBIRD!" We were off again. I started a story about a girl who loves leprechauns and meets one named Mr. Leppi, flying in her yard. Two weeks later I only had half a draft and thought I might send it unfinished, so Carly could feel, "I can do that too!" I waited, hoping she'd send me hers, and when I didn't hear by the end of the month, I emailed her: "Who should go first this time?"

"You!" she said again. The next day I was at her house, and she told me: "I like the story except for the girl's name, Sylvie, is too old-fashioned!"

"What should it be?"

"Hannah," she said.

"That sounds old-fashioned to me," I said.

"Becka," she said, which we both liked. Our first feedback session had gone very well! I thought. Perhaps we'd join forces in the adventures of Becka and Mr. Leppi.

Her poem or story didn't come, and two days into the new month, my daughter called. Carly was embarrassed to tell me that she was too busy to write something; she had too much schoolwork. "Maybe during the summer," I emailed her.

"Okay," she answered.

Did I intimidate her with half of a four-page story? She had shown me one from third grade that was eight pages, so was it really her busy schedule? She did have school, tennis, ballet, and play dates—

all filling the time needed to sit and look quietly out her bedroom window and muse.

I thought of myself at her age and how I stopped writing for fun the year after I won the prize for my story of a girl in a thunderstorm. My teacher put it in the school newspaper, and I was proud, but I didn't write another story until Mr. Plotkin's creative writing class in high school. After that, I stopped again until ten years after grad school.

What happened? Book reports, term papers, and analytic essays happened with their strict rules for conveying information, analyzing it, and comparing and contrasting. Without using I. None of my teachers wrote "Too creative!" in the margins and handed me a C+, which is what my students tell me happened to them in middle school and high school. I remember only the strong emphasis on writing with control, the opposite of writing to discover, which I need to say something I care about.

Plus, the more I studied great writers, the more I thought: "I can never do that!" and the louder the Criticizer in my head, saying, "This is no good! What others do is better." It stopped me from risking what I didn't know, listening for what I couldn't hear.

In high school, those who wanted to be "The Poets" wore beatnik black with long earrings and quirky caps. My neck was too short for long earrings, so I joined the high school newspaper as sports and ad writer, gained confidence in academic writing, and that's what I did until I was thirty-two. Then, on our sabbatical in the Middle East, I found myself with four hours of free time every day. The kids were in school, I didn't know anyone, barely spoke the language— and so I began writing about being "An American Abroad." When the local paper, *The Packet*, published it as a three-part series, and people responded, I remembered the writer I had wanted to be. My muse came back, or maybe she was there all along, and I just stopped looking through her.

In the Picasso Museum in Barcelona, the first room contains Picasso's work when he was eight or nine, before he formally entered art school. His sketches were full of whimsy—mythic kings, bullfights, and dogs—that filled his world before he absorbed the great medieval, classical, and Renaissance art. But many rooms later—after his Blue Period, Rose Period, Cubist explorations, and all the other movements he took in and made into his own—the paintings in the last room echoed the themes and spirit of his boyhood, deepened but still there.

Most of us don't risk a Picasso journey back to the creative freshness we had as children. Instead, we label ourselves "uncreative" or too busy with other things. "If you try memoir and personal essays, you can change that label," I tell my students on day one, and read them the diary of Opal Whiteley, a six-year-old orphan in a logging camp in Oregon at the turn of the century. I found it in Gabriele Rico's *Writing the Natural Way.*

Today the grandpa dug potatoes in the field
I followed along after.
I picked them up and piled them in iles.
Some of them were very plump.
And all the time I was picking up potatoes
I did have conversations with them.
To some potatoes I did tell about
My hospital in the near woods
And all the little folk in it
And how much prayers and sons
And mentholatum helps them to have well feels.

To other potatoes I did talk about my friends—
How the crow, Lars Porsena,
Does have a fondness for collecting things,
How Aphrodite, the mother pig, has a fondness
For chocolate creams.
How my dear pig, Peter Paul Rubens, wears a
Little bell coming to my cathedral service.

Potatoes are very interesting folks.
I think they must see a lot
Of what is going on in the earth.
They have so many eyes.
Too, I did have thinks
Of all their growing days
There in the ground,
And all the things they did hear.

And after, I did count the eyes
Their every potato did have,
And their numbers were in blessings.

The grammar is incorrect, the rules flaunted, and yet Opal makes us see the potato *her way* forever. My students begin to think: "If she can do it, so can I!" and good things happen that use "I" for discovery.

I hope that Carly will hold onto the gift from her first Muse to keep seeing the world anew. And that teachers will give great assignments to keep her creative sparks alive among the book reports. And that she and I will begin our email exchanges again—so that she keeps finding what I lost for many years: the quiet space and daring to listen, wonder, and imagine in purple, maybe with hummingbirds.

My Z Man

When Howie, my brother-in-law at IBM, offered to get me a new
ThinkPad at a great discount, I said no thanks. "I am going with Z
Corp."[1] He was amazed. "But why? I'll bring it to your house and set
it up for you." True, I liked my old IBM laptop, but Z Corp would
send a Z Man to my house within three days for a problem. A special
warranty, according to the sales rep.

And when my CD got stuck in its slot six weeks later, sure enough
my Z Man arrived the next day to replace it, one two three. "You see!"
I told Stu gleefully, as he stood in the doorway of my study, slump-
shouldered. He liked being in charge of all things mechanical, from
the broken hi-fi he said "worked" to computer crises, no matter how
many times the screen monitor warned him: "You have committed a
fatal error!" My Z Man meant independence for Luddite me.

Eight months later, a sonorous voice on the phone told me: "I want
you to take out the battery." I was speaking to Tech Support because
my laptop had died.

---

1 Any resemblance to corporations, living or dead, is purely coincidental! The name
   Z Corp, alas, is the only invented fact in this story!

"But where's my Z Man? He's supposed to do that."

"You have to do the diagnostics before we can send him," boomed the voice, like Moses on Mount Sinai.

"I didn't have to do that in New Jersey." It was midsummer, our family was at our lake house in New Hampshire—and I had a book deadline.

"Well, that's the regulation," the voice repeated.

I flipped the machine, and after much coaching, I located the correct black box and slid the battery case into my hand.

"Okay, good! Now take out the hard drive and then the memory."

The hard drive? A friend said she lost everything she wrote doing that. "I'm sorry, no way! My Z Man is under warranty; he *has* to come."

"You have to finish the diagnostics first, ma'am. That's our policy."

I hung up, fuming at corporate duplicity. What about those #1 in service ads? I muttered and swore until Stu came home and offered to call Tech Support back and work under the guy's instruction. I said he was crazy. If he destroyed my computer, decades of a marriage was over. My Z Man's contract was up after three years.

I hatched Plan B: to threaten a lawsuit *and* warn that I write about consumer affairs! Stu said not to bother. "They are used to that." An hour of phone fury later, I switched to Plan C: seduction of a lilting voice named Gavin. What seemed like thirty minutes later, I asked, "So could I have your supervisor?" and after "One moment, please," I heard another lilting voice named Jim, who sounded exactly like Gavin. I said I had crippling arthritis of the hands (Plan D), and when I mentioned the American Disabilities Act, Gavin/Jim came through. He would send my Z Man.

I raised my instantly healed fists, YES, and gave Gavin/Jim my summer address, reminding him twice that I was in New Hampshire, not New Jersey where I bought the Z. I canceled all plans, joyful.

No one showed. Two days later, on a hunch, I called my New Jersey number and sure enough, my Z Man had left two messages that he was on the way. Three calls later, I told a voice—maybe a person, maybe a computer?—that I was in New Hampshire. The Z Man will be there, I was assured by the lilting-voiced supervisor of a supervisor.

"Where?" I asked to confirm again.

"To New Jersey!"

"No!" I shrieked. "I'm in N-e-w H-a-m-p-s-h-i-r-e. Just give me the phone number, I will call myself!"

"I can't," he lilted.

"Why not?"

"Because I am in Mumbai."

I laughed like the maniac I'd become. India! India! Of course, recalling the endless hours spent on conveying the service tag number: T as in Tom, not V as in Vera. Z as in Zebra, not V as in Vera.

Chuck of Mumbai assured me he would take care of everything. So did Kelly from Idaho (My God, so close!!) and the brilliant Tim from Tennessee (two days later), who finally changed my purchasing address in the system "so the computer won't get confused."

Mike, New Hampshire's sturdy Z Man, arrived in a black-and-blue checkerboard shirt with a motherboard in hand. Calmly, he turned on the machine, heard a fan whirr and die, and said, "It probably isn't the motherboard!" Fifty screws later he was on the phone, ordering a processor, which, he assured me, would be shipped Air Express.

"So you are really coming back tomorrow? It is two hours round-trip."

"Yup." If I owned Z stock, I would have sold it.

Stu, suppressing his I-told-you-so grin, offered to lend me his old IBM ThinkPad. When the new processor also didn't work, and Mike had to order a video card, I tried to become Zen-like and did what I always do in crisis: write about it.

The video card didn't work, and Mike ordered a starter button. If that doesn't work, he assured me, Z Corp will you send a refurbished computer.

"Refurbished? But I am under warranty."

"Doesn't matter."

"I don't want someone else's reject," I told Carl from South Carolina, sweetly. This was feeling like corporate phone sex. "What I want . . ." I imitated the cheery voice on the Z Corp Main Menu, "is a NEW machine!" I added solemnly that the computer center at my college said I should definitely be given one under the circumstances.

"You bet! I would want one too," said Carl, with a charming southern drawl that sounded so real, I wanted to cry. "This kind of delay is terrible," he empathized. I responded to this fellow American by telling the details of my laptop's death over three weeks ago and how Z Corp, like Scrooge, sent parts one by one when the only chance for these machines, according to Mike, was to replace all parts at once.

"Well, *that* I just might be able to arrange for you."

I was smitten. This Carl sounded as if he could actually make a decision. He gave me his five-digit extension to prove he was there for me. "And if these parts don't work?"

"I'll send you a new machine."

I hung up, orgiastic, until Stu asked, "Are you sure he didn't mean refurbished?"

I ignored him, affirming my vows of loyalty to my Z Men—Mike the Real and Carl the Virtual—who would come through.

The next day a Raymond called to say one part was delayed and would arrive in five to seven working days.

"What part?"

"The motherboard."

"Excuse me? Did you say a billion-dollar computer company was out of motherboards? May I ask why?"

"I'm sorry, madam. I'm just the Information Provider. I'm happy to connect you to Customer Service."

The last time I spoke to Customer Service, Norma told me her division did not handle computer problems. I asked what else Customer Service could do in a computer company that received 1,200 repair calls a week in my part of New Hampshire alone. I got those numbers from Mike's boss.

"We do lots of things," she snapped, and put me on hold until I hung up.

Raymond from Information Service really wanted me to dial the extension number for "Very, Very Concerned Customers." I perked up. "Do you have one for Very, Very, Very Concerned Customers?"

"No, just Very, Very." He sounded so dejected, I dialed the five digits for the "Very, Verys," and heard, "If you know your party's five-digit extension . . ." I hung up. Ring. "Welcome to Z Corp, if you know your party's . . ." I hung up *again*. Ring. "Please press #1." Slam. I was sure it would ring in the middle of the night. Stalked by a main menu for the Very, Verys.

"It's not the motherboard," said Carl from South Carolina when I told him Raymond's news. "It's the video card that won't be available until August 15."

"That's three weeks away!"

"We discontinued your model and have to find, or make, a video card for it."

"My computer isn't even a year old!"

"Oh, we change models every six to eight months. The 5000 became the 7100 became the 8200. But what you get will be of equal quality or better," said Carl, still soothing with his Southern drawl. "Probably a 4150."

"But that number is lower!"

Not to worry, he assured. "I'll try to find a video card faster."

"But I want a *new* machine!" my voice rising. He understood, of course, but his boss wanted us to try these parts first. I demanded to speak to him. "She's away and will call you tomorrow." Great, I said, and added, lilting with the best of them, "And will you mention . . . just to be fair and up front, that I've written all three Z Corp co-presidents and the president." I was not bluffing. After the Norma episode, I called the public library, got all the CEO names, their real-world addresses, and went to the post office with four white envelopes marked "Urgent! Open at Once."

Two days later, things began to pop. Tim from Tennessee resurfaced and said a new computer would arrive within three working days. I imagined my Southern battalion fighting for me and called to thank Carl from South Carolina—but he was still searching for my video card. The next day Air Express (Now *that* was the stock to buy!!) brought a new (???) Z laptop, and that night I got a call from Tony in Z Corp's executive office, giving me his five-digit number *and his email* "in case you have any problems *at all.*"

I'd found snail mail power in a virtual world! So what were the magic lines? My cover letter?

> Dear Sir,
>
> When I buy a Z Computer with the promise of three-day "#1 service" in my home, why do I have to become a "computer surgeon" and take a computer apart first?

Or was it the opening for this essay?

> When Howie, my brother-in-law at IBM, offered to get me a new ThinkPad at a great discount, I said no thanks. "I am going with Z Corp!" He was amazed. "But why? I'll bring it to your house and set it up for you."

Whatever. I had the right template for future corporate transactions: insert whatever two names fit the occasion—GE vs. Westinghouse, United vs. American, Honda vs. Saab—and bingo. Six years later, it is still my best weapon.

The new computer had new wonders. It no longer required my begging for a Z Man, according to a funny little guy who danced across the screen. Not my type really, but hey! This machine had a built-in, 24-hour service if you clicked F1, which I did: "Hello, I'm Merlin the Wizard, and if you need me, I'll be right here."

The next morning I found out that Merlin was a limited wizard, even a troublemaker. Carl and Tim, the Southern battalion, no longer answered their five-digit extensions. And Tony, from executive offices, was on vacation, said his secretary. All I could do was to send him this email and hope for the best:

Dear Tony,

Thanks for replacing my 5000 with a 4150. All seems well except for three problems:

1. My machine turns on by itself in the middle of the night despite careful review of shutdown instructions (Merlin?).
2. I think my battery is dead.
3. I just received a bill from Z Corp to pay $1000 for this new machine.

Please advise . . .

Who Will I Be in Your Story?

A colleague of mine, let's call him Harry, told me what others have said over the years: "I'm worried about you being a writer. I'll end up in your book!" I laughed. His intuition was good. That morning, in fact, I'd begun writing about an incident at our college, and he, a.k.a. Harry, appeared on page two. "I haven't lost a friend yet!" I assured him, and mostly that's true, because I often avoid real names—and change identifying details as needed. I once changed my sister Ruth, always litigious, to Cousin Dora in *Thoughts from a Queen-Sized Bed*, and the first time I did so, I added this footnote:

> To protect the privacy of friends and relatives I've changed names and some locations, but the rest is true, as I see it.

Ruth called me when the book came out, delighted that "I got our family just right." She was certain that Cousin Dora was really Cousin Anne; I did not correct her.

Most of my readers, I've found, don't care whether I use real names as long as I signal name changes with "Let's call him (or her) . . ." or a footnote or initials. I did get one indignant phone call from my friend J.L. after she read my essay about lunch with a close friend,

"Anna," announcing her divorce. "I've known you for thirty years," she said, "and you never once mentioned Anna!"

"You're Anna!" I said, "At least part of you." This was the 1970s when marriages were breaking up left and right. I'd had the same conversation with three friends that year, so I combined them for privacy's sake, using a footnote. "The story was more about me than Anna," I said, "and besides I figured no one would talk to me otherwise." She laughed, saw the light; we made a date for lunch.

Of course, when I write about my family, Stu and my children, I have no choice; I have to use their names. So I clear my draft with them before publication, giving up a little editorial power for goodwill with those I want to keep in my life. My daughter, Julie, once corrected her dress size; Stu once asked me to cut the line about his eating cornflakes at midnight with a not-to-be-named syrup. All doable requests, partly because mostly they are minor; partly because I hear my version of Annie Dillard's warning in my head: While memoir is an art, it's not a martial art.

Memoirs about celebrities depend on naming. In Katharine Graham's *Personal History*, for example, the rich and powerful all sit at her dining room table—John Kennedy, Lyndon Johnson, Warren Buffet—all named. We read her book, even fifteen years later, to have a seat at that table, an inside scoop on what they thought and said off the record.

Memoirs about the infamous, as in Richard Hoffman's *Half the House*, also require naming. He rightly names the soccer coach Tom Feifel, who sexually abused him and other boys on Feifel's team in Allentown, Pennsylvania. This memoir broke the silence of shame; the other boys, now grown men, stepped forward, and Feifel went to jail. His real name mattered to bear witness, to expose—and also, as Hoffman points out, to protect the reputations of the other coaches in Allentown at that time.

But when a student read her essay in class about her gay roommate who had not come out, I started asking: Why use a name when it is harmful and there is no good reason? Why not change names and identifying details as needed? If that undercuts the story's integrity, then they should share the draft and get permission. Or switch to fiction with its "what if" possibilities and the chance to say, "I made that up!"

My friend, a former journalist for the *Washington Post*, told me he would never invent names or disguise identifying details. He was writing a book about his Amish neighbors at the same time that I was writing *Good Neighbors, Bad Times*, about Christians and Jews in my father's German village remembering Nazi times. I had decided to rename the village and the people, and he argued against that. "Truth is truth," he said. "Names matter."

"But if there are no heroes or villains, why not preserve privacy, especially when people trust you?" I wrote about that in my introduction:

> I realized that my subjects, who were in their seventies or older, kept thinking my book was only about the facts: the who, what, when, where and how of their lives. What they didn't realize, no matter how often I explained, is that I wanted their personalities to come alive on the page so that readers would meet them and discover as I did: who they were in their memories, who they are now, and how they struggled between those old and new selves.

Closer to his publication date, my journalist friend had second thoughts. Realizing he might cause trouble for his Amish neighbors in their community, he decided to give them anonymity. The book is *Plain Secrets*; the author is Joe Mackall—and I checked with him before using his name. He read the draft, made two small corrections, and said fine, adding that he also changed all the horses' names "because everyone knew everyone's horses."

I didn't need Joe's name for this anecdote. "My journalist friend" would have sufficed, so I left the decision to Joe. I do that only after asking myself two questions: Is the name essential to my story? What harm or good will come of it? The answers are always case-by-case, made each time I write.

Reading the newspaper, I wonder how journalists and their editors make decisions about names, especially when quoting everyday people who live in dangerous neighborhoods like Syria, Iraq, and Afghanistan. First and last names are often given (I assume they are real); and even if only the first name is used, some identifying detail is added: he works in a bakery, she teaches school. Sometimes there is a photo. Why put these people at risk? They are not heads of state; they wield no power; their quotes add local opinion and flavor, but do not shape events.

Like the Afghan resident, quoted in the *New York Times* about life under the lawless local militias after the American troops pulled out:

> "We are shivering with fear," said one resident, Abdul Ahad. Then he explained: He and his neighbors did not fear the Taliban nearly as much as they did their protectors, Rahimulmah's militiamen, who have turned to kidnappings and extortion.[1]

It was a front-page news story. What if some warlord has a cousin in the United States who sends him this article, translated? I would have been content with a quotation from Abdul or even from "a veteran farmer" or "a grim-faced student." I didn't need his name to trust what he said, especially when there was no consequence for others. His remarks could hurt no one except himself.

"It is a moral dilemma, but we can't be seen as protecting folks," says John Timpane, features editor of the *Philadelphia Inquirer*. "Our policy is to use real names at all times with a rare humanitarian exception." I had called John, a friend, to check my assumptions about Abdul Ahad. Do editors worry about people like him? "Newspapers would lose credibility, and if we protect one, why not all?" he adds,

---

1   "After U.S. Exit, Rough Justice of Afghan Militias," *New York Times*, March 17, 2015.

and besides, journalists don't know these people. "Maybe Abdul is a good guy, maybe not. We don't know someone's backstory, and we have a deadline in two hours." That, I realize, is a big difference between journalists and those of us writing first-person nonfiction. We have time to assess the backstory.

And we are also more focused on the universality of the moment than on reporting. I felt no need to name the school where I perceived an anti-Semitic incident—or the computer company that gave me so much grief. In part, because of the advice from a panel of legal advisers at an AWP writers' conference: "You want to spend your time writing, not in a lawyer's office." In part, because naming one school or corporation would let the others off the hook: "That's X, but we are Y. It couldn't happen here."

My friend, a.k.a Harry, told me that the movie *Whiplash* is based on the band teacher at the high school that our kids attended. The writer, Damien Chazelle, played the drums in a band class taught by a guy with a reputation for being severe and tough, but not the sadist in the movie. Damien calls his script fiction, making no claim that the real story happened that way. But if the real teacher was as mean and terrifying as portrayed, then I say call it nonfiction—and name him.

It matters, not like the name of my friend—who may be Harry, Bernie, or Bob.

In the Land of Double Narrative

We are in the Olive Room of the King David Hotel in Jerusalem for a meeting with two history teachers—an Israeli and a Palestinian—who have written a double narrative of this land. The Israeli, Eyal Naveh, in his open-necked shirt, has a casual toughness you find in many Israelis over sixty, yet with keen, blue-gray eyes that are empathetic despite his having fought seven wars to defend his right to stand here.

We don't know what his Palestinian co-author looks like, because he is on the speakerphone. After waiting two hours at the checkpoint, Dr. Sami Adwan knew he'd never make this meeting and returned home to Bethlehem. "This is typical of the problem here," says Naveh. "I was stuck in traffic; that is all right. My Palestinian colleague was stuck at the checkpoint. That is not all right."

Our group of thirty-five sigh and nod. We are lawyers, entrepreneurs, peace activists, professors, political operatives, and writers, mostly American and many Jewish, on a ten-day, fact-finding trip to Israel, the West Bank, and Jordan. Our host is J Street, an American organization committed to a two-state solution to the Palestinian/Israeli crisis, one with strong security for Israel and a viable state for the Palestinians.

I'm here, in part, because of a photograph over my desk: of my father visiting Mount Scopus in Jerusalem in 1924, one of hundreds who watched the ceremony of laying the cornerstone of Hebrew University and imagined a Jewish democracy built on justice and fairness. I also liked the J Street itinerary. We are meeting all sides: from Israel's president, to the Palestinian Authority's prime minister, to Jewish settlers, to West Bank resistance fighters, to UN officials in Gaza. "A whiplash trip," is how Jeremy Ben-Ami, the head of J Street, described it. And so it is, each voice informing and contradicting the next as we sit in the same room. Except for two Palestinians who had to cancel because of checkpoint issues.

So today's hitch is not a fluke; it is part of the double narrative of this land. You hear it in words like *The Nakba*, or Catastrophe, which is how Palestinians describe the first war in 1947, the one the Israelis call *The War of Independence* because it began after the Arabs rejected the UN pronouncement of the State of Israel—and attacked. And in what the Israelis call *The Security Wall*, designed to stop the suicide bombers from blowing up discos in Tel Aviv and bus stations in Jerusalem—and the Palestinians call *The Racist* or *Apartheid Wall* because it cuts into their land and prevents their moving freely into Israel proper for jobs and family, as they did before the intifada, a word that conjures up the liberation movement for Palestinians and the existential threat of annihilation for Israelis.

The book that Naveh and Adwan wrote, together with two other scholar/activists, is called *Learning Each Other's Historical Narrative: Palestinians and Israelis.*[1] It begins:

> Schoolchildren studying history in times of war or conflict learn only one side of the story—their own—which is, of course, considered to be the 'right' one.

They wanted to correct the way "one side's hero is the other side's monster," so, in 2002, after the Oslo Accords, they recruited twelve

---

1   Dan Baron (Israeli) and Adnan Musallom (Palestinian).

teachers to try out the double narrative text in their ninth- and tenth-grade classes. The Israeli version is on the left:

> The war . . . is known as the War of Independence because it resulted in independence for the Jewish community in the land of Israel, in spite of the fact that at the beginning local Arabs, and then armies from Arab countries . . . attacked isolated Jewish communities, Jews in the cities with mixed populations and roads. They also employed terror tactics—all Jewish people, settlements and property were considered to be legitimate targets.

The Palestinian version, on the right:

> Fighting and clashes between the Jews and the Palestinians began after UN Resolution 181 was passed by the General Assembly on November 29, 1947. The situation deteriorated into an unequal confrontation. Zionist forces were organized, armed and trained. Not only were they superior to the Palestinians, who for over 30 years had been exhausted by unjust British policy and Zionist terrorism, but these gangs were also superior to the Arab armies which entered the war on May 15, 1948.

And in between is white space for students to join the conversation. Naveh tells us that people are ordering the book around the world, but you won't find it in Israeli or Palestinian schools because of politics on both sides.[2] "No permission yet, but we keep trying," says Adwan on the speakerphone.

Such a book could get beyond the sound bites of vengeance and fear, our group agrees. It could promote understanding and empathy. *If only* . . . I think of a line attributed to Napoleon: that "history is myth that men agree to believe in" and how the double narrative undercuts that myth—and all else that depends on telling one side of the story.

---

2 It is published by PRIME (Peace Research Institute in the Middle East) and can be ordered online.

It is the oldest of stories—and begins with Abraham, the patriarch, coming from Ur (somewhere in Iraq) to the land of Canaan (now Israel/Palestine) with his wife, Sarah. They are childless for so long that Sarah, beyond the age of childbirth, agrees to let Hagar, her Egyptian handmaiden, have a child with Abraham. His name is Ishmael. Years pass and, miraculously, Sarah gives birth to Isaac.

Jews, Christians, and Muslims agree on this, even about God testing Abraham's devotion by commanding him to go to the mountain and sacrifice his only son. But then comes one word—Isaac—and the story splits apart.

> Take your son, your only son, Isaac, whom you love and go to the region of Moriah. Sacrifice him there as a burnt offering on one of the mountains I will tell you about." (Genesis 22:3–212).

"We believe it wasn't Isaac but Ishmael who was to be sacrificed by Abraham," said Dr. C., a Pakistani Muslim who taught "Understanding Islam," a ten-week course I took at the Evergreen Forum in Princeton before this trip. The course's aim was to promote interfaith understanding and dialogue. "Ishmael was 'the only son.' Isaac wasn't even born yet." The Jews and Christians in class flinched. This was not our story. Genesis says "Isaac," and we believed it. "And what's more," Dr. C. continued, "unlike Isaac, who struggles against his fate, Ishmael goes willingly to God. In fact he volunteers. So it is written in the Qu'ran."

That night, I reread Genesis and found no signs of Isaac struggling. In fact, Isaac was duped. When he asks Abraham where the burnt offering for sacrifice is, Abraham says, "God will provide." Nothing more.

I read on to another problem: God's double promise. First, there's the covenant with Abraham that Isaac, and his descendants, will inherit the land, which is why religious Jews claim both sides of the Jordan River as their birthright:

And I will give to you, and to your offspring after you, the land where you are now an alien, all the land of Canaan, for a perpetual holding, and I will be their God.

But God also promises that Ishmael will rule. After Ishmael and his mother Hagar are expelled from Abraham's camp and dying of thirst in the wilderness, God says, through the Angel of Death:

Come lift the boy up and hold him fast with your hand and I will make a great nation of him. (Genesis: 28:18)

And then a well of water appears.

Muslims reenact this part of the story every year in Mecca, said Dr. C. with pride. "I myself took part." He told us how, dressed in a plain, white loincloth like the other pilgrims on the hajj, he circled seven times as Hagar did "until Allah, Blessed Be He, was convinced of her devotion and made water miraculously appear."

When Abraham dies, Isaac *and* Ishmael return to Hebron to bury him next to Sarah. I didn't know about that until Dr. C. showed us a PBS film about the three great faiths. I liked the question asked by one of the Christian theologians in the film: "Is it the beginning of a new story or the end of an old one?" He didn't know, but I saw reconciliation in the two heads bowed, side-by-side—and wished this were the scene we all reimagined, and told our children.

Our bus takes the settlers' road that bypasses the checkpoint with its long line of trucks and cars and heads for Hebron, the West Bank's biggest city. Our guide, Ilana, is a passionately peppy Israeli-American in her late twenties who leads an organization dedicated to bringing Jews to the West Bank to see life through Palestinian eyes.

Ilana points out the Wall and the expanding Jewish settlements that have exclusive rights to this road, so Palestinians can't drive on it. She points to the water towers, some white, some black. Palestinians often have their water shut off by the Israelis and so need extra water tanks on their roofs for storage. Those are the black ones. Israeli settlers don't have these problems and have one tank, in white. "That's how you tell who is who in this occupied land."

And yet, looking out the bus window, I am struck by the lush countryside, the neat rows of vineyards, bright white houses, and fields of olive and fruit trees. Whether it's from foreign aid or the Palestinian Authority's growing power to keep order in the West Bank, Palestinian life in 2010—despite Jewish settlements, some rising like fortresses—looks thriving, even prosperous.

We stop on the edge of Hebron, at the Cave of the Patriarchs, where Abraham and Sarah are allegedly buried, along with Isaac and other founding mothers and fathers of Judaism, Christianity, and Islam. Abraham, the Bible says, paid good money for this spot: 400 silver shekels to Ephron the Hittite, turning down a free burial site. As an outsider, Abraham must have wanted proof of ownership:

> So Ephron's field in Machpelah near Mamre—both the field and the cave in it, and all the trees within the borders of the field was deeded to Abraham as his property in the presence of all the Hittites who had come to the gate of the city. (Genesis: 23:17)

It was about real estate, even then.

We don't go inside the Cave of the Patriarchs—this is not that kind of trip—so I don't see the subterranean caves or the places where Jews, Muslims, and Christians have, alternating over the centuries, come to pray. Ilana's focus is on the Israeli soldiers standing on Shuhada Street that abuts the Cave complex. "Israel needs five hundred soldiers to protect six hundred settlers and two hundred rabbinical students. Why? Because they live in this Arab neighborhood." Several of us shake our heads. What a waste!

The Israeli soldiers, less than a dozen, are heavily armed and solemn. No one smiles or waves, the way I remember in a younger Israel.

It was 1972, the year my family spent a sabbatical year in Haifa. Israel had taken over the West Bank in the 1967 war, but the moral and political ambiguity of occupation had not yet set in. We hiked with Israeli friends in the Jordan Valley, we shopped freely in Arab souks in the Old City of Jerusalem, and the army stood guard, holding a moral compass that pointed one way: to defend Israel's right to exist. We all felt proud of the soldiers, and they felt proud of themselves, smiling easily.

"Can you imagine?" Ilana says. "This was once a thriving Arab marketplace." She looks down the long street of boarded-up stalls. Except for one souvenir stand, it's like a ghost town from a movie set. An old man and a child walk toward us, single file, along a narrow walkway defined by concrete barriers. Someone says, "apartheid," and Ilana points to the checkpoint at the other end of the street. I ask one of Ilana's helpers, a red-bearded rabbinical student from Jerusalem, where the people of Hebron shop now that this market-place is closed. He shrugs. "Nowhere."

"Did the shop owners get compensated at least?" Another shrug.

Across the road from the shuttered stalls is a long wall of murals. "This was once a thriving bus station," says Ilana, adding that the Jewish settlers put the murals up. She moves on. I stop to study the colorful pastel scene of Hassidic Jews on crowded streets and read the heading: "Christians and Jews are welcome to live here as they did in the old city of Hebron." No Arabs though.

The wall's history is in four parts, beginning with the "Roots of the Jewish People." Here in Hebron, it says, our forefathers and mothers are buried. Here is the capital of Judea, where King David began his reign. And here in 1929 "Arab marauders slaughter the Jews. The community is uprooted and destroyed." There is a plaque with two candles and a picture of a rabbi and his wife, among the sixty-seven or more killed in those riots. The British, then in control, evicted the remaining Jews, wanting no more trouble here.

The last mural has the heading "Liberation, Return, and Rebuilding" and beneath it: "1967: liberation of Hebron and reestablishment of the Jewish community." Ethnic cleansing pops into my head, which I resist. Yet what else to call it when a people are wiped out of Hebron after centuries of living here? A sign leans against the high, stone wall:

> "This land was stolen by Arabs following the murder of 67 Hebron Jews in 1929. We demand justice! Return our property to us!"

The lettering is in bright red, full of fury and self-righteousness. I recoil from the certainty of hate.

Ilana, it turns out, told only half the story when she blames the Jews for taking over this Arab neighborhood. Before 1929, it was a Jewish neighborhood; the settlers are arguing for the right of return, much like the Palestinians who had to flee Jaffa and Ramallah in 1947. It's ironic how, in the heart of the double narrative, the themes are the same: displacement, exile, right of return, victimhood, injustice.

"Before 1929," says Herzl, a psychiatrist from Wisconsin who is part of our group, "Jews and Arabs lived in peace. "In fact, my grandparents were rescued by Arab neighbors during the 1929 riots." I want to know more, but we get separated at the checkpoint line. Instead I hear others behind me:

"Wasn't Hebron where the bloodiest riots of the intifada took place?"

"Wasn't that rabbi killed here?"

"Yes, and then that Goldstein guy slaughtered twenty-nine Muslims who were praying at the Ibrahimi Mosque . . ."

Ilana interrupts to point out four Arab schoolgirls in blue uniforms. "They must pass through the checkpoint twice, to and from school—and until recently, they had to go through an X-ray machine. Some parents were so concerned about radiation, they kept the children home." We feel their parental despair—with outrage.

Half a block beyond the checkpoint, everything changes. We are in the middle of a bustling marketplace, both modern and timeless.

There are rows of bright yellow buses and cabs, windowed storefronts, and streets packed with stalls of goods piled high with blue jeans, embroidered dresses, pita, and shoes. There's even one with string beans. Why isn't this part of Ilana's story? Does it lessen the impact of the empty street? Or the Arab schoolgirls? Not for me. I'm drawn to the gray narratives, the contradictory truths: the deserted souk and the thriving marketplace; the evils of the Occupation and the Massacre of Jews in 1929. And now, a third narrative told by Herzl of Jewish rescue by Arab neighbors. How can there be peace without revealing it all?

"This restaurant is Hebron's best," says the assistant mayor, who greets us in a room full of lattices strung with grapevines, the sunrays streaming in. Each table has two Palestinians who will tell their story, says Ilana, as we sit down to mounds of hummus, pita, and black olives, all the good stuff. Beside me is a young Palestinian teacher, slim and earnest, who speaks excellent English and says, shyly, that he spent a few months in the United States. I'm about to ask where, when the mayor stands to welcome us. An urbane man in Western dress, he tells us how important it is for us to be here together. "Even the Jews among us should feel welcome," he says. I wince.

Then Herzl stands up—it's his turn to introduce our group and say how pleased we are to be here. People keep dipping into hummus, familiar with the routine until we hear, "This day is special for me because my family comes from Hebron." The restaurant quiets. The mayor's contingent looks up. We all do, as Herzl tells how his grandmother was one of the four hundred Jews who were hidden by twenty-eight Arab families during the massacre of 1929.

His great-grandparents came to Hebron from Eastern Europe in the 1800s, very religious people. They multiplied and prospered, he says, until 1929 when those who survived had to leave. He pauses, his voice shaky with emotion. "I am the first of the family to come back here, to break bread with you whose families may have saved my grandmother and others in my family. To you I want to say thanks." You could hear a pin drop. Stories like this, of people on the other side being decent, are rarely told, for they fit no one's political agenda. And yet without them, how can we correct "one side's hero is the other side's monster"?

I ask Herzl why he didn't dwell on those who were killed, because the descendants of the murderers were probably also in the room. Yes, he says. "But that wasn't what I wanted to think about. Dwelling on victimhood only leads to victimhood." After Herzl speaks, we hear from three young Palestinian men who have come to the same conclusion. They are part of the growing Arab movement that sees nonviolent resistance as the best way to gain a Palestinian state. Ali, a handsome, brooding man with an electric smile, comes "from a family of fighters" (Israelis would say "terrorists"). He and his mother have been in Israeli jails, his brother was shot by Israeli soldiers, and yet he has turned anguish and fury into a peace-focused political strategy. "Being pro one side is not enough. You must be pro solution," he says. Jews must like his message, for Ali is often invited to speak. "I never knew I'd be in so many synagogues, speaking as I do here today."

After the official program, I talk with the young Palestinian beside me. He grew up on a small farm next to a Jewish settlement and says there was a hole in the barbed wire fence between them. He and the Israeli children would crawl through, trading marbles for figs and plums. To this day, his family has a photo in their farmhouse of both families together at some shared celebration. During the intifada, the fence was patched; there's no interaction anymore. I ask what it would take to change that. "Take down the fence," he says. Simple, really, when the answer comes out of individual experience that contradicts the one-sided narrative.

From my window in the Intercontinental Hotel, I see a mosque below me, the afternoon light glowing red on its stone. Not much movement. Has it been abandoned? I ask the Israeli concierge, who thinks it may be used sometimes. He doesn't know its name. When I go to the hotel pool, full of bikinis and voluptuous white towels, I imagine the muezzin's call to prayer, maybe even hear its low murmur on the other side of this stucco wall.

To the right of the mosque, are Tel Aviv's beaches: white sand and calm blue sea, at least from up here. To the left is a building with its back against the sea, containing a semicircle, like a small stadium. Every Israeli knows what's here: the burnt shell of the Dolphin Disco blown up by a suicide bomber in 2001. They know twenty-one Israelis, mostly teenagers, were killed and one hundred twenty were wounded. They know there were many other attempts to bomb it—and that a Palestinian terrorist group claimed responsibility for its "success." And after this tragedy, the Israeli army tightened security, increased checkpoints and made building the Security Wall a priority. Nine years later, enemy rockets are still falling on the borders with Gaza and Lebanon, but no suicide bombers have gotten through again to this heart of Israel.

The name of the mosque is Hassan Bek. Before 1947 it was an important mosque, but after many Arabs fled, it sat idle until Israeli developers made plans for this site. Then the Muslim community in Jaffa, Israeli citizens all, joined together to restore the mosque as a place of worship. It has become a symbol of their rights as Israeli Arabs in the future Israel. Will they be respected? Will they be knocked down?

In the States we had a great debate about a proposed mosque so close to Ground Zero. The memories of victims collided with the rights of those who, fairly or not, are seen as guilty by association. America may be a big enough place with a short enough history to absorb such a clash. But in this small land, there is no room to maneuver; ground zero is everywhere you stand.

I am on the midnight flight home from Amman, laptop open at 2 a.m. writing about Jordan:

Today we met King Abdullah and Queen Rania, and what a Camelot couple they are. She is beautiful, a Palestinian, who talked with great enthusiasm about building schools and health centers. He, urbane and savvy, seems most willing to articulate both sides of the conflict. Is it because he is across the border?

The guy beside me touches my sleeve. "Will you send me a copy of what you are writing?" He's dark, slim, and Mediterranean-looking, with a tiny scar on his cheek—and an appealing earnestness as he hands me a slip of paper: "Abdul O_" neatly handwritten, with an email address below it. "I was looking over your shoulder and want to read more." He smiles. "You are writing about my king." Abdul lives in Florida now, a U.S. citizen, he says, but with family still in Jordan.

I'd like to keep writing, use this time to sort out the many voices we heard, all interesting, all persuasive, but this man continues. He tells me how he was born in Saudi Arabia, grew up in Amman, but his roots are in Hebron. "I am a Palestinian," he says solemnly, "and I tell my three children the same!" His family left Hebron in 1937, the same year my father left Germany, I realize. Which is probably why, when he asks me where my roots are, I answer "Germany" instead of "New York," my usual response. "My parents left because of Hitler."

He nods. "You are Jewish."

"Yes," I say. He nods again.

Now I could shut my computer and then my eyes, as on other long flights next to strangers who keep talking. But here is a Palestinian who is not royalty, not in the high-powered political loop we've been in all week—and yet an essential part of the story. "Why do you still feel Palestinian?" I ask.

"Roots are roots. Do you not identify as a German?" He immediately rethinks. "No," he says before I can shrug, "I can understand why not."

Again, a place to stop talking—except he says, "My family once saved a Jewish family. My grandmother would often tell the story of what she and my grandfather did."

Now I am really engaged. "Was it during the massacre of Jews in 1929?" I pause before the word 'massacre,' not wanting to offend with ten more flight hours to go. Abdul shrugs. "I don't know when exactly, maybe it was 1929. I only know the family story."

I can't help it. I imagine Abdul's grandparents saving Herzl's grandfather and think: How great would that be! I scan the aisle looking for Herzl's silver hair and firm jaw; he is somewhere on this plane.

"Have you been back to Hebron recently?" I wonder if he has seen the Israeli soldiers on Shuhada Street and the empty stalls.

"No, the last of my family left under the Jordan rule, a difficult time. But the family house . . . Maybe, Allah be praised, it is there. I'd like my children to see it one day."

Abdul returns to the story of rescue. "My grandmother said a Jewish family came to the door, saying, 'Please save us!' So my grandfather took them to the basement and hid them. If someone comes to your door for help, it is written in the Qur'an that you must help."

I wish friendship rather than religion had made the difference, but I won't quibble. In my father's German village, during Nazi times, Christians brought soup at night to hungry Jews, someone shared a ration card, another saved a Torah, but in dozens of interviews, no one mentioned standing up to anyone, let alone to a mob outside the door.

"There was a Jewish man on our trip whose family had lived in Hebron for generations." I say, "and his grandfather was rescued in 1929 by Arab neighbors. In fact he's on this airplane!"

"Is that him?" Abdul points to heavyset man in a black T-shirt who asked me for the pretzel snack I wasn't eating. I shake my head, turning to look for Herzl one more time. "I don't see him."

Abdul now shifts from past to present. He is a computer programmer who has suffered an aneurysm, so he's on medical leave. And his three-year-old daughter has diabetes since birth, and he must give her shots of insulin every day. He was never religious, he says, but now goes to the mosque daily to pray for her. He takes out her picture, a sweet, chubby child, and I see tears in Abdul's eyes. "I would gladly give up my life for her to have a good one. Why not? I've been all over the world, I've done so much." I doubt he is older than forty and think how powerful is his willingness to sacrifice his life. "She's adorable. I wish all the best for her and for you." He sits up. "Whatever is God's will," he says, and thanks me. "You are kind."

We become less cautious—and talk about the settlers taking over Palestinian land. Terrible, he says, and I agree. We talk about the checkpoints. He says they stop people from earning a living, and I agree. "If this region has peace, I think the whole world would have peace," Abdul says, and I very comfortably challenge what I hear as the subtext that if Israel went away, everything would fall into place. "What about the Shias and Sunnis?" I ask. "They will battle without the Israelis."

"You are right. This is a problem," he says.

"What about Hamas and Hezbollah?" I ask. "Israel can't pretend they are not there."

Abdul says the same thing that Prime Minister Fayyad of the Palestinian Authority told us: "These groups will lose power if there is peace." We are on the same track, nodding, pleasant, sensible. And then out of the blue: "You know what created Hamas?" his voice rising now. "The Americans! You know what created Hezbollah? The Israelis!" I hear the words bounce off the ceiling. Whoa! I can't let that go by, another version of the blame game, that everything is everyone else's fault.

"I don't believe this to be true," I say, telling him, lecturelike, that Palestinians must also take responsibility. "Everyone must give a little to build trust on small issues before the big problems can be tackled." His eyes glaze over. "It's like in marriage," I say. "My husband hates when I leave my shoes in the bathroom. If he complains nicely, I'm more likely to say, 'Sure, I can fix that . . .'" Abdul's eyes light up. "You are right. It's the same with my wife, only I am the messy one!"

We venture below the "We all want peace!" mantra until anger builds, we are quiet for a while, and then we start again. Maybe because I know about his daughter, and he knows about my marriage, even about my shoes.

Waiting for our baggage at JFK Airport, I see Herzl. I tell him about Abdul and how he has a family story about saving a Jewish family. "Where is he?" Herzl asks, with great excitement. "I must talk to him." At first I can't find Abdul among the hundreds waiting, but then I spot him, a smaller man than I thought, not someone you'd notice in his black chinos, dark shirt, unhurried. He must have a long layover. "There he is!" I say. "Next to the cart with the boy sitting on a green trunk." Herzl hurries over. They talk. I see Abdul smile. I can't see Herzl's face, until he walks back to me, all smiles. "I am so happy you told me that," Herzl says, and, taking a deep breath, whispers loudly, "I told him thank you."

Baggage in hand, we get ready for home or other flights, but for a moment we relish the common ground we've found to stand on— and the small narrative we all can tell.

PART 4

Border Crossings

One crosses the border to become a new person.

—YIYUN LI

Ad In, Ad Out

I love being someone who charges the net for a midcourt slam and surprises with an ace, now and then. Which is why a fact I never bothered mentioning at twenty, forty, or sixty, is now my shibboleth: "I'm a tennis player." When people look me over and say, "Wow! You *still* play!" I feel powerful in the world.

I said it first at physical therapy, after my back went out for the third time. I was lying on a mat beside an older woman spread out like a dish towel over a large red ball. She had been coming to PT for six months, she said cheerfully, three times a week. "I'm a tennis player," I said emphatically and rolled my pelvis five times, pressing my spine to the floor, as I was instructed. I moved closer to the young guy on the other mat, who was doing leg crossovers. "Two herniated discs," he said with resignation. He'd been coming here for a year. "It's better one week, worse the next."

"I'm a tennis player," I assured him, as if I were off to a tournament. He was in his forties, my son's age, and had time to waste. I, the tennis player on Medicare, did not.

The trainer came over.

"If you show me all the exercises, I'll do them at home," I said, annoying him. He wanted me, and my sciatica, to come for thirty-two weeks, the length of my insurance coverage.

"You need supervision for these exercises."

"Don't you have diagrams that I can follow?"

"Yes, but even with . . ."

"I'll be fine," I said.

Two months later I was fine. Not from his exercises, but from the one I got from Jane, a perky woman in her sixties, whom I met while playing tennis despite a pain across my butt. "Oh, try this!" she said in the ladies locker room and got down on the rug to show me the exercise that saved her. Relax, flatten your spine and bend one leg. Put the other across it, push bent knee out, pull ankle in and work up to thirty seconds. Switch legs. Do it twice.

I got down, tried it and heard a crunch; well actually a series of clicks. I was sure I would never rise again, but I did. And my spine opened up, liberating a nerve. "If I do them every morning—and after tennis," she assured me, "I'm fine." Four months later, on the floor and in position, I listen to clicks every morning, but not as many. No more sciatica.

This exercise heads my list of top medical advice given for free. Others include: 1) Eat yogurt if you are taking antibiotics (from my college roommate). 2) Rub the inside of a banana peel on psoriasis (from an attendant in a bathroom). 3) Take vitamin C (from almost everyone I know who is not a doctor).

I did give up playing singles, except for Heidi. She is fifteen years younger, but doesn't mind playing for only an hour. She teaches aerobics beforehand and Zumba afterwards, and on the days when she rides her bike ten miles to the courts, I can beat her.

My friends Mike and Sam, both over eighty, have weekly tennis games playing singles and doubles. Their secret, they say, is to play by Mike's Rules: 1) Hit the ball to the other person. 2) Don't keep score. 3) Consider all aces as do-overs. 4) Ditto for missed return of serve that lands in the net. Both men are lean and well preserved, an inspiring sight that I attribute to tennis. Good exercise gets every-thing going, true; but even healthier, says Mike, "is the idea of being a contender, of still being in the game." The aim is not to win but to keep the ball in play with as many good shots as you can.

What *I* don't want is to start looping the ball, the way the old ladies do on the next court every Tuesday. That's what our group calls them—"the old ladies"—because every movement is careful and awkward. I want grace. Worse, whenever the pace of their game picks up, someone lobs to slow things down. I want speed. One day in the locker room, two of the "old" ladies were beside me, and I saw that in their street clothes, they were, in fact, around my age. That's when I decided that as soon as I start playing as if part of me might break with my next step, I'll take up *tai chi* or walk a few miles on the canal, to hell with tennis.

The worry is: how to know when? A woman in my doubles group for thirty years, a fine player until two years ago, began losing every week. She told us she hadn't been playing enough, needed to take a lesson or two, was having cataract surgery, couldn't get over the flu. Someone suggested that she try a less competitive game, but she wanted none of that. She will be back to her old game, she kept assuring us with apology—until last week. After losing 0–6 with three different partners, she said, "Well, at least we all got good exercise!" My kinder self was sympathetic. "It will happen to all of us one day." My competitive self fumed *We have to know when to quit.* I recently read about how the part of the brain that cares what others think gets weaker with age. We will all go from *I'm sorry!* to *Who cares?* That is hard on grace.

My mother gave up bridge because of the tremor in her hands. Two years earlier when her eyesight dimmed, her fellow bridge players bought an oversized deck so she could see the cards; but within a year she was constantly dropping her cards. Did they stop inviting her or did she give bridge up by herself? She never said, but I could see her hurt as her world closed around her. She kept on knitting by feel, but her sweaters never fit as well. And her amazing potato bread, *Berches*, wasn't as golden as before.

I still love her needlepoints, especially the giant, blue dragon, the size of our couch, skimming on low waves of blues and white across our living room wall. Museum quality, its stitching so fine that the dragon took her a year to make, and she was my age.

What stunned me was how proud she was of the canvas she dragged out of her closet soon after she turned ninety-one. "Surprise, Mim-la, and Happy Birthday!" she said, as I stared at four dull red-and-brown figures playing four sports—tennis, golf, soccer, and basketball—in stitches so loopy the knots showed through. *She didn't do that! Someone far less talented must have stitched for her!* I thought, kissing her in disbelief. I put the giant thing in the windowless bunkroom of our lake house, hours away. It was painful to look at, but how could I throw her determination away?

Some days I lose at tennis, 3–6, 2–6, like today. I'm not worried, I decide, while sitting on the couch under Mom's dragon after tennis. I've had game scores like this before, even as a kid. *I didn't move enough, the lights glared, I didn't have enough sleep last night.* I make a tennis lesson to work on my volley. Maybe I'll have two. Whatever I need to pick up my pace and keep leaning toward the ball, however hard and fast it comes.

On Stage and Off

Man is a make-believe animal . . . never so
truly himself as when . . . acting a part.
—WILLIAM HAZLITT

Broadway. My name in lights. It all seemed possible, sitting in the last row of Forest Hills High auditorium, waiting to audition for Play Pro, the drama club. I knew my soliloquy cold as Linda, the wife in *Death of a Salesman*, having said it perfectly in the shower three times that morning:

His name was never in the paper. He's not the finest character that ever lived. But he's a human being, and a terrible thing is happening to him. So attention must be paid.

It didn't help. I fled to the bathroom before my name was called, right after my best friend was too good at performing Juliet to her unseen Romeo.

Maybe if the school librarian had given *me* Juliet, or Emily, the girl in *Our Town*, I would have climbed the three steps to the stage. But at sixteen, with big dreams and a new boyfriend named Stu, I couldn't imagine myself as a widow my mother's age, full of fierce grief. All I imagined were my arms hanging down awkwardly like a gorilla's.

In Mr. Plotkin's English class, I wrote a short story about an evil ferret, and everyone loved it, so "Mim, failed actress" switched to "writer." And that stuck—until a friend, fifty-two years later, asked me to join OnStage, a group of closet actors, all over fifty-five, that met weekly with a local director, Adam Immerwahr, to learn theater techniques. "We also gather stories from the community and perform them locally as scenes and monologues, each year on a different theme," she said. "It's called documentary theater, because our 'scripts' are the stories real people tell us in interviews. We record them, and Adam transforms them into our roles. Kind of like Anna Deavere Smith." I'd seen her *Twilight: Los Angeles,* 1992, a one-woman play of those telling her about the LA race riots. "Last year," my friend continues, "OnStage did 'First Jobs'; this year it's 'Thriving, Not Just Surviving.'"

I had recently retired from full-time teaching, finished a book tour and was looking for something new. Yes, I'd started a novel called *Solo,* about a long-married couple. Not Stu and me, more like my parents. But ever since Stu's cardiologist said he needed a defibrillator implant, I'd been cleaning out closets rather than write past page forty.

"Sure!" I told my friend, out of the blue. "If OnStage is fun, I'm in!" I liked the idea of weekly theater games and performing "scripts" that were like stories you hear over lunch or on a bus. *If not now, when?* I thought, and forgot my gorilla arms. The pressures of youth were off.

In the Community Room, we play "Name a Scene"—the beach, a garage, the top of Mount Everest—and I converse with the clamshell, or mechanic, or Sherpa beside me. I never know which until my partner moves or says something that I have to answer. Whatever comes out, it sticks—with no revisions. Such a nice break from writing!

I also work on *Yes, and,* which is so much better than *No, but.* To refute someone, according to Adam, will stop an improvisation cold. So if A says to B, "It looks like a hot day," and B answers, "It won't last!" there is silence. Nothing more to say. But if B answers, "*Yes, and*

I'm going to sit on this bench all morning!" all sorts of possibilities arise. "*Yes, and* will you sit here tomorrow too?" "*Yes, and* I am going to sit here beside you." Maybe said sweetly, maybe with menace. Either way a story begins.

The week after learning *Yes, and,* one woman from our group came in with an epiphany. "All my life I've been a *No, but* person. This week I've been totally *Yes, and.* What a difference it's made! I got everything I wanted!" My own epiphany came from another theater technique: GOTE, which got rid of Stu's pile of books on the floor. GOTE stands for Goals, Obstacles, Tactics, and Expectations, and on stage you must use them all. Say I'm a shoplifter and want a candy bar (Goal), but the store clerk keeps eyeing me (Obstacle). I start choking so that he'll get me some water (Tactic), and I think I'm safe *if* I can get past the cop who's buying coffee (Expectation).

Here's how GOTE worked for me:

After years of nagging Stu, "Your books clutter the floor . . . I trip on them . . . You are not reading them anyway . . . Don't be such a jerk . . ." I'd gotten silence, annoyance, and an occasional "I'll get to it later." Post-GOTE, I smile in victory every time I get in and out of bed. All it took was:

Honey, could you remove those books [G]? I know you are reading them [O] so I made room on the shelf in the hall [T].

Stu looked at the books, looked at the shelf, and within minutes he put them there, gone from the bedroom corner for good. Where had GOTE been during the four decades of our marriage?

The best is when I lose myself in a character whose monologue I've memorized. Words take me over without my permission, and suddenly I become the ditsy thirty-five-year-old who is super-eager to get the job at a medical insurance agency "because I want to help people." My Ingrid (that's what I name her) is oblivious to the boss looking at the marble ceiling, tapping his desk, and saying snidely: "We'll be in touch!" I, Mimi, would have noticed, but my Ingrid leans forward optimistically: "Did I get the job?" I would have stomped out the door.

Some characters enjoy what I don't, like the mom (I name her Leila, from Kansas), recently retired, who is knitting her daughter a shawl. I hate knitting, probably because my mother knitted tons of sweaters for everyone, and too many sat in my closet unworn. Leila loves it and loves having time to garden, which I would never willingly do. And she is so very earnest: "I had a lot of responsibility on my job. I'd even stay up at night thinking about it." I'd never say that out loud. And she keeps repeating herself: "before I retired" followed by "when I retired."

The writer in me wants to cut and tighten—to make her good lines zing, so they don't sink under phrases such as "different shapes and patterns":

> In the fall I go into the garden and look at the leaves, all the different shapes and patterns, and there are still flowers left and I know I won't see them again until the spring so I want to remember.

I offer to rewrite the weak lines, and Adam says: "That's how someone actually said it! You must find the character who would say it that way." (He will rearrange and cut the stories we gather in recorded interviews, but won't change the words.) I love not sitting at the computer, deciding what's good and what comes next.

Next I become the reluctant grandma (I name her Beatrice from Brooklyn) in a scene when she announces that she's not going on another family "Beach Week." The beds are too uncomfortable, the car ride too long: "You go, have a good time," says Beatrice to her daughter. "I just don't feel like it anymore." I'm into this part, with lines I've felt but never said.

The daughter tries flattery. "But, Mom, what about your pasta sauce . . . that everyone adores?"

"It's from a jar, okay?" says Beatrice. "I used to let it simmer for three days, now it's Ragu. Face it, the magic is gone." The daughter dials the grandchild and, with a sly grin, hands over the cell phone to a reluctant Beatrice:

Hi sweetie . . . Yes, I heard you got a new pail, but listen . . . Yes, and a new shovel too . . . Listen, grandma is really sorry but . . . Yes, I want to see you swim underwater.

Of course, Beatrice ends with "When we get in the car tomorrow, will you sit in the back with me?" What else is there to say? I think of our two-year-old granddaughter looking at a peach, wow, or throwing a ball into the lake. wow. It's so easy to get hooked by joy, thank God.

I'm given a new monologue to learn on the day Stu is going again to his cardiologist. He's having trouble breathing; even walking to the street corner is hard. Maybe it's a fixable problem; we hope so. I am to play a widow, trying to explain how life has changed since she's living alone. "I don't think I can do this," I tell Adam, "especially if my husband gets a bad report from his doctor. He is there today."

"Try it out!" Adam says. "Just to see."

Stu comes back with new pills that should work, and I start learning the lines, silently. To say them out loud with Stu in the house feels like a betrayal or worse, an invitation. A friend once wrote a poem that imagined her child's death; I couldn't take such a chance.

I try a Southern accent, so as not to be me—and name her Isabella from South Carolina, picturing a sturdy Southern widow, maybe with Yankee stock somewhere. In the shower I straighten her Yankee back and say with a drawl,

When I think about my family now, it's very small and contracted. With the loss of my husband, my whole world is contracted. Astonishingly so!

I linger on the *r*'s, the "very" becomes "verry," and I continue on, getting more comfortable with each repetition—the hot water pounding, the bathroom door shut with Isabella inside.

The woman who really told this story is a New Yorker. We sat in a story circle together, passing the microphone around as each of us responded to the prompt: Tell something about family. I knew her husband too. He had died three years earlier after a long and solid marriage, and she talked of her sorrow and vulnerability openly, more than I could ever risk. So I'm grateful that Adam tells us not to imitate the person if we know who told the story: "Just find a plausible character that might say the words. You have a range of emotional options."

In the supermarket I meet a woman in my book group and think *She is my Isabella!* Her husband died in early spring. He had the same problem as Stu, congestive heart failure, and last winter standing at the ATM, she and I talked about the danger of breathing in cold air. I had sent her the website address where I bought Stu a hood to get through the winter.

"How's it going?" I ask her. We are in the cereal aisle in front of Bisquick and McCann's oatmeal. "I'm doing well," and she looks well. Her white hair is neatly coiffed as always, no random strands of contradiction. Her trench coat, tied securely at the waist, looks fresh from the cleaners, unlike my rumpled ski jacket. Here is a strong woman, carrying on, not staying at home in tears, which is how I imagine myself as a widow. "It's a little hard figuring out what brands to buy." She is scanning all the shelves. "My husband did the shopping." Suddenly the depth of her grief is there, pushing against the will for normalcy, to keep going with her cart down the aisle. Which she does. I decide not to give up my part as Isabella.

The next morning I am in the kitchen rehearsing, while Stu is upstairs taking a shower. Each time I say the lines, something eases in me, the repetition inoculating me, not from disaster but from overpowering fear. I'm glad that I must keep becoming Isabella, who shuns dark rooms and unending tears. And then Stu walks in with more bounce than yesterday, wearing his blue shirt, my favorite. I stop in midsentence.

"Do you know your lines?" he asks.

"Want to test me?" The words come out as if nothing about them is dangerous, just words in a kitchen of moving light angling off the table.

"Let me have breakfast first." It's what he says whenever I waylay him first thing in the morning to listen to a first draft I've written. Only the first few paragraphs, enough for him to pronounce: "I like it" or "I don't know" or "So so." How to fix the problem is not his thing, but I've learned after years of muttering *What does an engineering professor know!* that he is uncannily right about when I am phony or whiny or hedging. Maybe because we met when we were sixteen and guileless, before we knew who we'd become. People say marriages that start when you are young don't last because individuals change so much; but change can make a marriage work, adding variety and a way out of ruts. Stu says he's been married ten times to someone named Mimi. I say at least five times to a boy named Stu. With each new role—becoming parents, my teaching far from home, Stu's rising career, his heart attack, my breast cancer—we've somehow said *Yes, and* in time.

Stu finishes his yogurt and fruit. "So let's hear your new role." I thought he forgot and that I was off the hook of gloom.

"It's close to the bone," I warn. "I'm playing a widow describing her life alone. I don't know if I can get through it—or if you want to hear it."

"Go ahead," he says, folding the newspaper.
I begin: "When I think of family now . . ." I watch his face, searching for a set jaw, grim lips, and the words feel wrong. It's still Mimi in our kitchen, self-conscious and scared—until I say "verry small." I start to disappear and by "with the loss of my husband, my whole life contracted," Isabella has taken over: "People say it must be like losin'

your right arm." She raises my right arm. But it's not like losin' your right arm, 'cause when you lose your right arm, you still have your left arm you can work with. Now she raises my left arm, our back straight as can be. I don't cry, don't break down, don't even flub my lines:

> It's when those fingers are intertwined so that they're stronger together, then the loss of your spouse, if it's a good marriage, just leaves a space between your fingers that isn't verry strong and isn't . . . Well, it just isn't.

Isabella is not asking for pity. She pushes against the grief:

> It's a very strange evolution one has to get accustomed to. But I keep tryin' and I'll win. Well, eventually, I'll lose when they shovel me under. But I'll keep tryin'.

I say these lines as Isabella many times before Stu dies, and then afterwards. I do it to be back in this kitchen as Stu applauds. We hug; it's going to be okay, maybe, we hope. I touch his forehead; the same strand of hair keeps falling down. And yes, there are tears we don't try to avoid as he refills his chamomile mango tea and says with the generosity I count on: "It's good. You should do it."

Lessons from a Last Day

Stu's living will is in his backpack when he checks into the little New England hospital near the lake house where we stay every summer. Not that we are worried. He's had mild pneumonia twice before, a side effect of a weakened heart. The slight fever of the night before didn't stop him from playing Mexican Train with his granddaughter Sara, the white-tiled dominoes standing and falling with their laughter, her delight being his.

It is only the threat of Hurricane Irene, one day away, that keeps us from going back to the lake house with oral antibiotics, as before. "With your heart condition," the clinic doctor warned, "if you run into trouble, and the trees are down, you might not get here in time." "Besides," he added, "IV antibiotics work more quickly than pills." With a big family party coming up next weekend, "quickly" sounded good, so Stu agreed, and now, a few minutes later, in comes the wheelchair. Stu backs away. "I'll walk, thanks. I'm fine!" The nurse, a blonde with a winning smile, says, "Oh, come on, handsome!" and he climbs cheerfully on, and they chat nonstop as she rolls him down the hall that connects clinic to hospital.

I stay to fill out forms, and when I get to Stu's room, he's already in bed. A dark-haired young man is in the middle of the room, introducing himself.

"I'm the hospitalist," he says in a clipped accent that sounds from Pakistan or Iran.

"What's that?" I ask. He turns towards me.

"The hospitalist handles in-patient care." Dr. K is the name written on his white jacket. "I am in charge of your husband's treatment."

I try to loosen him up with a smile; Stu tries joking about the Red Sox game. No luck. So Stu says: "Just give him the living will—and the health proxy." We had started keeping copies in the glove compartment, just in case, so that the list of end-of-life protocols we *don't* want—resuscitation, antibiotics, oxygen, forced feeding—would protect us, insuring death with dignity. Not like my grandmother who spent ten years in a nursing home, blind and senile, because paramedics jumpstarted her heart at eighty-nine. Or like Stu's aunt who, despite severe Alzheimer's, had both legs amputated at eighty-six, a week before she died.

The hospitalist glances at the documents and gives them back. "So do you want the IV for intravenous antibiotics, or not?" He sounds annoyed with us.

"Of course, that's why we're here!"

"And should we do everything we can?"

"Of course, this is mild pneumonia, right?"

"Mild pneumonia, absolutely. But still I must ask." He writes something on the chart. What, I find out only later.

Stu asks for his backpack and gives Dr. K his traveling medical record—a four-inch-thick history of cardioversions, ablations, EKGs, and echocardiograms since his heart attack in 1988—all ordered and backed by data on an Excel sheet. That's what engineering professors do. I hand this over along with Dr. R's cell phone number. "He's the cardiologist my husband sees up here. I called him, and he says you can call anytime, and he'll fill you in." Dr. R is connected to the big hospital, thirty miles north, and we thought of driving there until the local clinic doctor said: "You'll wait in the ER forever. Here you'll be hooked up to antibiotics within an hour."

Not quite. The hospitalist first wants an echocardiogram, an EKG, and the results from blood work, so when our son comes two hours later, after his daughter's swim lesson, the nurse is just starting antibiotics plus oxygen, because Stu is feeling worse. Alan immediately asks about transferring Stu to the big hospital, but the hospitalist keeps saying, "It's just mild pneumonia. The antibiotics will soon kick in."

"What did Dr. R say when you called?" I ask.

"I haven't called yet. Too busy." *This place is almost empty.*

"But he's expecting your call." *You have time to order extra tests,* I'd love to shout, *but not to call the doctor who knows Stu's heart?* But I need this hospitalist who has the power; we have no advocate here. At home in New Jersey, Stu's doctor came every day after Stu's emergency appendectomy in May; he read his charts, adjusted his meds, and kibitzed, as the two men have been doing for twenty years. If there was a hospitalist on duty, he made no difference to us.

By evening Stu is feeling more chipper—and eating a cranberry scone that Alan brought. We all like Stu's nurse, a lively brunette who seems charmed by this upbeat, silver-haired, seventy-two-year-old patient.

"Go home. Get some rest! I'm going to sleep," Stu tells me, and the nurse nods in agreement. So I leave, but when I call in the middle of the night, she tells me, "He's uncomfortable." I hurry back, taking the curves of our moonless dirt road as in daylight.

"Hi!" I say ten minutes later, as if I always drop by at 3 a.m.

"Hi!" Stu says, with effort. "You're here." His breath is raspy, and I begin rubbing his back in large circles of rhythm, as I did when he was in intensive care for three days after his heart attack. For twenty-two years we have believed backrubs have saved him. "Umm. That's good!" Stu's breathing steadies, and my fingertips find his spine and climb to his shoulders. "Keep that up all night!" He smiles, and so do I—until he can't seem to get comfortable lying down.

Stu's nurse used to be a cardiac nurse at the big hospital. She props more pillows under him and whispers to both of us: "You could make a formal request to transfer." Nurses, I've found, know everything and tell you the truth, so I leave to look for the hospitalist. He's chatting at the nurses' station, and I say, trying to be calmly authoritative: "I'm requesting that my husband be transferred to the big hospital. It is better equipped, and his cardiologist is there."

The hospitalist scowls. He doubts that the hospital will admit anyone who is not an emergency, not with the hurricane coming. "Your husband is fine." And no, he hasn't contacted Dr. R yet.

The sun is up when Alan arrives. His family is going back to Boston—school starts this week—but Alan says he'll stay awhile. I don't remember when the questions start. A small catheter would improve the delivery of antibiotics. Do we agree? Of course, if it will help. An intubation would help the breathing. Do we agree? I'm not sure what intubation involves, but yes, of course, if it will help. Stu is having more trouble breathing, and dozes more, but we still believe in mild pneumonia. No one says not to.

In fact, I don't really worry until—*Is it an hour later, three?*—Stu's nurse comes over and hugs me, saying, "I'm so sorry." And then another nurse comes over and squeezes my hand. *What is happening?* Alan rushes to find the hospitalist, who has disappeared and then reappears, announcing, "I have ordered a helicopter to fly the patient to a crisis center. This hospital is no longer equipped for your husband's condition."

Words I have pushed away since 3 a.m. suddenly take over: that Stu could die—not in a vague sometime, but now. For years I've rehearsed "what if" scenarios, with every thud upstairs, every phone call when Stu travels alone. I never rehearsed what I now say in panic to Alan: "Maybe we should keep Dad here. Maybe we should just make him comfortable. Maybe you should call your sister." Julie is out west on vacation, and mild pneumonia hasn't seemed worth calling about. Alan nods, and we hug each other longer than we ever have, afraid to say more and weep.

I want to be with Stu, feel him close, but they've moved him to the other side of a glass window. We are being kept outside, as four medics hover over him with pumps and tubes under harsh lights. Quick desperate moves that finally push me to ask: "What about hospice care?" The words feel like a betrayal and a gift. I know Stu wants no heroic measures when all hope is lost. But is that now? This hospitalist, this Dr. K, has offered only optimism, so how can he have Stu strapped on a stretcher about to fly away from me? There is no room left onboard.

"Hospice is not an option," says Dr. K. Two men are wheeling Stu through a doorway. "We have no beds or personnel for that."

"But my husband has a living will. It allows us to decide what to do. You saw it and read it." I try again to sound like Stu, in charge. People listen to him, but he can decide nothing now, so I, with his medical proxy, must make his choices.

The living will became void, says the hospitalist, when permission was given to treat pneumonia with IV antibiotics. A total misinterpretation, two lawyers tell me later, but it led to Dr. K writing "Do everything!" on Stu's chart. And that's what the staff has been doing.

"My husband wasn't in crisis; there was no emergency. He just had mild pneumonia. You kept saying that." No matter. "But it's a legal contract." No matter. I feel the voiceless fury of a dream. Stu has wishes and rights to dignity without futile end-of-life measures. Listen to them. Talk to me. No one is paying attention. No one is telling us whether his death might be happening. Or not.

Stu is flown by helicopter to the big hospital, while I drive like mad up the interstate to get there first. Alan is at the house getting my toothbrush so that I can stay overnight and keep rubbing Stu's back. We have hope, you see. Even driving north on the highway, I don't really think death. What I think of is Stu in the helicopter and how he hates a wild ride when he isn't in charge. After his heart attack in 1988, he'd tell everyone: "I knew *if* I survived the ambulance ride on the I-95 during rush hour, I would live."

Dr. R is waiting to take me to the Cardio Lab. "They resuscitated Stu three times with cardioversion procedures," he says softly. "I wanted you to be able to say good-bye." I try, with growing dread, to be grateful. Young doctors and nurses file out of the lab, leaving Stu and me among the machines, huge and humming. I stroke his hair; he does not speak. I kiss him, talk to him, convincing myself that he can hear me say *I love you.* That it isn't too late, that he didn't die in the air, alone.

"We were duped!" I tell my New Jersey internist a month later. She wants to know how I am, and I say I'm trying to keep busy and not sit in dark rooms. Much of my grief has turned from tears to rage at my helplessness on that August day. "All those tests and procedures—and Stu was dead within twenty-four hours." I feel violated by greed and arrogance. The daily barrage of hospital bills fuels my cynicism even though I have good health insurance: IV antibiotics, aspirin, echocardiograms, two in-house cardiologists we never saw, and $18,000 for the helicopter that flew Stu north to the big hospital two hours before he died. Or maybe he was already dead. Maybe the little New England hospital didn't want Stu as a death statistic—and shipped him out.

My internist is a card-carrying member of Compassion and Choices (that's one reason I picked her), so I don't expect her challenge of my outrage: "If there is even a 15 percent chance of saving a patient, you have to take it," she says. "Especially when things are changing quickly as often happens with older people." She suspects septicemia as the cause of Stu's death. Septicemia—a word I look up online:

A sudden severe infection . . . life threatening for those with weakened immune systems . . . often caused in hospitals.

Did septicemia kill Stu? Dr. R suspected it too, especially with Stu's immune system weakened by the emergency appendectomy three months earlier. Septicemia can move fast, especially in hospitals. Did he catch it there? I never found out because no one in the little hospital ever mentioned the word. Only pneumonia was mentioned as the cause of death.

What my internist—and every doctor I talk to—cannot understand is why the hospitalist didn't call Dr. R, Stu's cardiologist up there. "*We* emphasize collaboration," my internist says. A friend on Princeton Hospital's Ethics Board reinforces that idea: "Our hospitalists must contact the patient's doctor if at all possible."

"Perhaps in theory," I say, before telling him how my neighbor took her husband to our Princeton emergency room after the hospitalist in charge (yes, they are in New Jersey) refused to call the family doctor "because he doesn't have hospital privileges." My bioethicist friend can't believe it, investigates, and gives me a call. "A bad apple," he says. "That doctor was dismissed soon after."

Most hospitalists, I hope, are good apples because 42,000 now practice in American hospitals. We are all likely to find ourselves in their charge when we climb into a hospital bed. Why? The upside, I'm told, is that they are trained to coordinate hospital care and be more efficient. The downside, as Stu and I experienced, is that they don't know the patients, have no context, and rely heavily on records and tests. If we are lucky, the hospitalist will contact our regular doctor, but collaboration, though highly desirable, is not required.

It's been three years now, and I've come to terms, mostly, with end-of-life issues being messier than Stu and I thought when we signed living wills. And more complicated. Yes, there is a disconnect between ideal and real-time decisions. Yes, people often change their minds at the end of life. And yes, when things happen quickly, as with Stu, it's harder to enforce a living will than when dying is slow and more predictably timed, the way it was for my mother, dying at home of cancer, under excellent hospice care.

But one truth remains uncomplicated for me: the right to know what the doctors and nurses know *in real time.* How else, living will or not, can we know when mild pneumonia becomes septicemia, and death is no longer a long shot, but close at hand? I said yes to IV antibiotics, yes to oxygen, yes to a catheter—all Do Nots of the living will—because Stu had mild pneumonia; he was not dying. He would get well, and IV antibiotics were supposed to speed his recovery, better than antibiotic pills.

When did that change? Certainly before the nurses hugged me to say, "I'm so sorry." Was the hospitalist too afraid to tell me earlier? Too arrogant? Too embarrassed? Too unpracticed in delivering bad news? Or had he really convinced himself that our initial yes to IV antibiotics voided the living will and his responsibility to honor it?

Whatever the reason, I don't accept it. The only response I accept is what Dr. Besser, a wonderful doctor and friend, says he tells dying patients and their families. Often, more than once before families— sometimes angry, sometimes weeping, sometimes in denial—are able to hear his guidance:

> When I know, or even think, that there's little hope, I bring family and patient together and say, "Look, we can keep trying everything. Or we can make you as comfortable as possible so you can spend the precious time that's left quietly, together."

How I missed those words on Stu's last day. How I wanted someone with expertise and empathy to offer me options, make a recommen- dation, and then genuinely ask: "Should we make your husband comfortable or fly him to the big hospital?" I imagine myself saying, *Yes, yes. Make him comfortable*—but, of course, that's after Stu had died. On that day of fading hope, maybe I would have said, *Go quickly! Fly him there. Save him, do whatever it takes to keep him alive.* I don't know. I can't be sure.

But if it were today, the helicopter waiting, I would want to make that choice. And with the right doctor's help, one who accepts the fog of hope and hopelessness, I would have had enough time for holding hands and good whispers in the private quiet of letting go.

Lyrics and the Way We Love

When I was thirteen, I'd lie on my bed in Queens and listen to Doris Day sing about falling in love forever. She was pert and pretty, and so girl-next-door that her dreams became mine. By fourteen, I was waiting for a call from whatever amazing boy I had fallen in love with that week. And by sixteen, that amazing boy kept being the same boy. He was a year ahead of me in school, with broad shoulders, a low, sexy voice, and he never called too soon or too often. Was it because of basketball practice or calculus tests? Or did he somehow know that half of my excitement was in longing? Either way, I received what I needed: the slow buildup to a crescendo of romance in the Midway Theater balcony, his arm around me falling now and then to my breast. Not too quickly, not too hard—or else this Mr. Right, whose name was Stu, would turn into just another grubby kid whom I could not love forever.

Stu usually called Tuesday nights for Friday or Saturday, and if he was late, I'd stare at ceiling cracks over my bed and play "Blue Moon" without a dream in my heart. I was sure he'd never call again, no boy would because I was too bold, too shy, too talky, too fat. But the song continued, assuring me that my true love would appear, the only one my arms could ever hold. And it would last forever.

This is the promise of love I grew up on.

There were hints of the women's movement to come. Ethel Merman, with pistols on her hips, belted out that anything a guy could do, she'd do it better. My Mr. Right would have to consider that possibility. There were siren songs we fifties girls sang on girls' sleepovers. In pajamas, eating popcorn, we tried being seductively strong like Lola in *Damn Yankees.* Whatever she wanted, she got. And we sang bad-girl songs that felt dangerous and daring as we swayed to "Love for Sale," without a clue of what we were asking for.

Stu and I met in bio lab. He lent me his Parker pen, I broke it, he made me pay for it, and he asked me out to the movies. Afterwards we ate pepperoni pizza at Mama Sorrento's, and did so every weekend until we ended up dancing in my den to Frank Sinatra's "That Old Black Magic" and "Fly Me to the Moon." Stu's hard-on pressed against my thigh, as we moved from first base to second with the lure of third. That never happened with Nat King Cole or Perry Como; they were too much like Hallmark cards. Only Frank Sinatra with his edgy, come-what-may romance could seduce us with love's complexities and risks that we sensed without understanding—and liked them, come what may.

Nevertheless, we chose Doris Day's forever love as "our song" at our wedding six years later. Our bodies glided in sync before everyone we loved, Stu's hands pressed the small of my back, my breasts pressed his chest, as we whispered love *Till death do us part.* We were twenty-one and twenty-two.

In graduate school at the University of Michigan, as Freedom Riders headed south, we played Pete Seeger and Odetta for social justice, had two babies and got degrees. My first teaching contract arrived the same day as my pregnancy test results, so I stayed home while Stu studied on. Pregnancy was forbidden in classrooms of those days.

On the radio, Sinatra gave way to the Beatles singing about a girl with kaleidoscope eyes, and we got their gist. But when Dylan asked how it felt living on your own, like a rolling stone, we had no idea. We'd never had that chance, not like our kids, who would roll through their twenties uncommitted, settling down in their early thirties. I admitted to being a bit jealous; Stu did not.

When Julie and Alan became teenagers, love lyrics filled our house again. We were a two-career family, very short on time, but I paid attention when Diana Ross sang "Touch Me in the Morning" and James Taylor and Carole King wondered "Will You Still Love Me Tomorrow?" I hummed Carly Simon's "You're So Vain" after every argument over who forgot Stu's shirts at the cleaners and the dozen other chores we passed off on each other.

Stu liked the Bee Gees' "Staying Alive," but his favorite was "Wake Up Little Susie," rediscovered one New Year's Eve around our year twenty, when with strobe lights whirling, he danced like a wild man all night, full of young moves. He'd belt out "Wake Up Little Susie" every morning after that while taking a shower. I'd hear him downstairs in the kitchen.

Somehow we missed Leonard Cohen's songs. I think we heard "Suzanne by the River" and "So Long, Marianne" on the radio in the late 1960s and liked them, but never heard Cohen's name until a friend, who'd known him at McGill University in Montreal, gave us the double CD set of *The Essential Leonard Cohen* for our fiftieth anniversary. I fell for his velvet voice, with enough gravel; his earnestness, with enough irony. It put me back to the days of dancing two-step to Sinatra in my den, when we sensed a price for romance and moved our bodies closer. The Beatles could vow never to dance with another (whoooh), and you pictured them grinning. But when Cohen sings of love a thousand kisses deep, you are hooked, even knowing that the good-byes of "So Long, Marianne" come next, and all you can do is laugh and cry about it all.

We played *The Essential Leonard Cohen* for five hours, driving north to New Hampshire that last summer. His words kept touching a raw nerve of desire and loss, especially after Stu's emergency appendectomy had left him frail. We hoped a summer at the lake house would restore his weakened heart, so we could move forward. In "Dance Me to the End of Love," I longed for the touch to dance me safely through the panic. Would our dance last or was it ending?

I heard both as we passed Hartford, then Springfield where the air always clears, the sky bluer than before. I don't know which lyrics moved Stu most that day. Was it Suzanne who let you touch her perfect body? Or Marianne? Or "I'm Your Man"? Or the one that moved me most: about no one knowing where the night is going. *I need you. I don't need you. I need you.*

All Stu said was "Play him again." And I did.

I played the same CDs driving home in late August two days after Stu died. We had no real chance to say good-bye, and I was in shock. One day he was "good enough," as he'd joke when asked how he was feeling; the next, he was gone. Not the heart attack I always expected, but pneumonia that was mild until it wasn't. Stu's coffin was in a hearse somewhere on the same highway, but after yesterday's Hurricane Irene, flooding everything, who knew where?

Cohen's lyrics sounded so different. What I'd heard two months earlier as love and longing, now baited me with death. *Who by fire? Who by water? Who in the sunshine?* How easy a quick turn of the wheel going eighty would be! But then came "The Night Comes On," urging me back—go back into the world—and I hit the brake and cried for twenty or thirty miles.

Then the mystery of "Anthem" took me over.

Ring the bells that still can ring,
Forget your perfect offering
There is a crack in everything
That's how the light gets in.

Could it be? In one stanza I heard the refrain "That's how the *night* gets in" and kept playing the song again and again. *Light* or *Night,* I couldn't decide. They both worked as I drove on, needing to know.

Six months later in my young friend's SUV, her sons thump in the far back seats to the rhythms of a song that asks someone to blow a whistle. "Inappropriate!" says their mom. "I'm switching stations."

"Mom, I know all about that," the twelve-year-old assures her.

"Your brother doesn't. He's ten."

It was a Flo Rida song. "He's a rapper," the ten-year-old informs me, his fingers still tapping away, ignoring the new melody about soft white snowfalls.

I go online later to retrieve the lyrics of "Whistle" and realize it's about oral sex, the rapper assuring the girl he'll show her how and not rush her. At twelve, the only "inappropriate act" I knew was the disgusting French kiss. Blowing a guy's whistle was giving a wet kiss, but that was the world of 1950s decorum.

A month later, in my son's van, Taylor Swift is singing. My grand-daughters, twelve and four, know every word and belt out "I Knew You Were Trouble" with hip-hop movements executed with seat belts on. They sing as a team, with shoulders and bellies wiggling, that worst of all *wasn't losing him; it was losing me.* They are thinking self-identity, not like me at their age, lying on my bed mooning over being Mr. Right's sidekick.

The next song comes on, giving new twists to forever love. The singer is mad and quite ready to forget forever. It's not happening, they are not getting back together, ever. Swift sings tough, confident, neither a sexpot Lola nor Doris Day's girl next door.

My granddaughters' fingers point upwards, a scolding motion, and they are laughing more with each refrain. I wonder what promise they bring to their future from these lyrics about love.

The only "forever" love songs I hear are on Christian radio, which cuts into NPR while I am driving one day. God's love is reliable, sings voice after voice, sounding sweet and sexy. He will satisfy you, not like earthly lovers, who are temporary and fail you. I switch channels, and Justin Bieber is singing that he just needs somebody to love, as if anyone will do. Bruno Mars follows with "The Lazy Song," singing he's fine hanging out alone. He can curse and masturbate if he wants to, and tomorrow he'll think about meeting a girl, having sex so good she'll scream out how great it is, Oh god, Yeaaah! His who-cares ease reminds me of a fifties song, "Mañana," about how life now is "good enough for me"; the rest can wait. But that guy was singing about a leaky roof.

Online, I look up the favorite love songs of today and find Fantine singing "I Dreamed a Dream" from *Les Misérables*. She reminisces about a magic time when men were kind, love was blind, before life killed her dream of love. She is done dreaming, expecting nothing more, no blue moon promises of reappearing love.

In a comment section, a dozen women admit they can't stop weeping through this song, and I'm not surprised. What I don't expect is the young bride, smiling in white, her arms around her groom in a photo beside her comment: "I know every word in this song." No bridal optimism about forever for her; she seems primed for the worst. Which may be realistic, but I prefer my overdose on Doris Day's promises, that, until recently, led me not to notice her early warning (by line 3) of a restless world in which love ends before it's begun. And I sang the words since I was thirteen! That oversight may not have kept Stu and me together through ups and downs, but it didn't hurt. I think we take what we need from lyrics of love.

I pay the bills in Stu's study, surrounded by his bookshelves. His stacks of papers are gone from the floor, his orange couch gone, his ratty, torn rug replaced by me with a rope rug that looks better, but I hate its rough feel on my bare feet. His old rug was soft.

I come for Stu's music. Charlie Parker's jazz, Mozart's violin sonatas, Eliot Fisk on guitar playing Segovia. Just their sounds. I play nothing with words, hoping I can channel Stu's *You can do this, relax* as I check bank statements, file taxes, all the things I hate, which he did with ease. Robert Browning promised: "Who hears music feels his solitude peopled at once."

I want it true, especially after I had to erase Stu's voice on our answering machine, putting my voice over his *Have a nice day*, which made even grumpy people answer, *Have a nice day, too!* I had no choice. Stu was telling people to "please call Mimi and Stu in New Hampshire." If I had left it as is, no one would know what happened, where he was, where I am. On the day of the funeral, I replaced his voice with my *No one is here right now . . . Have a nice day!* and tried to match his spirit, but couldn't.

I'm in Stu's black swivel chair, opening a hospital bill from Stu's last day when "It Could Happen to You" comes on in a jazz set. Again no words, but I hear them anyway. It's Frank Sinatra, singing in my den in Forest Hills, and I wonder where Stu's arms could be. I start to hum, softly at first, and then sing every word as if we were together.

And it happened to me.

A Vine of Roses

A week after my mastectomy, my friend Penny sent me a gift that I shoved in the closet. It was a framed poster of a woman with one breast, her arms raised in victory to the sky. Across her scar is a vine tattoo. This was 1988 when the media had started to write about breast cancer, using titles with "tragedy" and "terror," signaling hysteria and doom. And this before the doctor found my lump. A woman with breast cancer was labeled "victim" or "survivor," and I remember no images. Visuals were far too shameful.

Yet here was this poster woman, not tragic but brazen—and I kept thinking about her when on day ten, I took off my bandages and confronted the jagged red scar. And again when my husband and I made love. And again when I started back to work. Within a month, the one-breasted woman was out of the closet and over my desk to look at every morning. I began saying, "I had breast cancer" instead of "I have breast cancer," even though I had no guarantees for anything.

I considered breast reconstruction, but then I heard of a neighbor ending up with uneven breasts and a cousin of someone having three surgeries because of a leaky saline implant. A tattoo fantasy—mine with a vine of tiny roses—seemed easier. I didn't seriously consider it because tattoos, back then, were for Hell's Angels and sailors in sleazy parlors on a street of bars. But I did whisper to my husband one night, "Maybe I'll get a tattoo on the scar!"

"Do it if you want," Stu said, kissing what was no longer there. "But you don't need one."

It was the perfect answer, along with the one when I wept after misplacing my prosthesis, and he went off calling, "Here, Titty, Titty!" Self-pity had no chance. Tears went to laughter and to trust. I didn't get a tattoo.

Twenty-five years later, my scar has faded to white, along with another over my belly button after a GI bleed (too much Advil), and I'm again thinking of tattoos to cover my scars. Since Stu died—it's been two years now—I'm trying to figure out my body without him. I've started to go to the movies and dinner with other men but intimacy seems like a leap. I miss curling around someone at night, but could I make love with the lights on and walk around casually naked in the morning? With one breast?

I'm reconsidering breast reconstruction, but then I should add a facelift, liposuction, tummy tucks, neck lift, the works. And I still won't look as new as the kitchen chairs I reupholstered. So no, I'll just stick to my rule about medical procedures, which is the same as for the comma: If in doubt, leave it out.

Yesterday I found a half-dozen websites displaying tattoos over mastectomies. Most are enormous, like the barn owl in pink and gray, its wings flying over half-hidden red leaves. And the blue arctic fox with its paw on a saved nipple, its tail draped over a bare shoulder. And a toga of giant pink flowers set on emerald leaves that wind their way from shoulder to scar to hip to butt. I would disappear in such designs, and I'd miss myself. Only one tattoo, "Bad Ass Chest Piece" done by Tina Bafaro, made me imagine possibilities. It's an Art Deco brassiere in swirling reds, blues, and browns that you'd never find in Victoria's Secret. The tattoo initially went viral, and Facebook shut it down, saying mastectomy tattoos are taboo. But it is back up again—and I saw it. We've at least come that far.

This morning I passed a young woman in a scooped-neck shirt, with "Brooklyn" tattooed like a banner across her chest. It's ironic how the generation that avoids commitment is fearless about such permanency. I, who lived with one man for fifty years, would worry: What if I move to Queens or Tokyo? Would I want my Brooklyn past so prominent for my life? I let the tattoo idea go again, thinking I'm too old and impatient. I can barely sit still for an occasional manicure; plus it would hurt, even a small tattoo like my vine.

Enter my four-year-old granddaughter Karen with a tiny rose on her arm. It's temporary, her mother assures me, taken from a book of tattoo designs she found at the toy store. An hour later, I'm in that store buying two books of tiny flowers, stars, hearts, and other joys of color no more than an inch big (including the princesses and white horses, which I will give to Karen).

Back at home, I choose a rainbow for my mastectomy scar and a blue rose for above my belly button, and, standing before the mirror, I peel, press with a damp towel for thirty seconds. And I am tattooed. I love them, these shifting shapes of self-definition. And when they fade three weeks later, I switch to a peace sign over my belly button and two roses where my left breast was. I leave space in between to show a pale scar of connection like a thin laundry line. History unhidden.

Fix-It Fantasy

When you're married, for fifty years, to a man named Stu who fancies himself as Mr. Fix-it (I say "fancies" because of a varying success rate), you don't learn how to hang pictures, unclog dehumidifiers, or replace toilet seats. So when, after a weekend of guests that include two uber-bathroom-going toddlers, you discover that your toilets' seats now roll like a ship on the high seas, you need to do something.

It happened six months after Stu died. I remembered his toolbox was on the workbench in the basement and went downstairs. But as soon as I saw it sitting there, I knew it was Pandora's Box, able to unleash a grief I could not easily put back. Like the day I moved Stu's bike to the back of the garage. Or realized his Cheerios were stale. Small moments, so unpredictable, not like Thanksgiving or death certificates for which I was ready.

I phoned my friend's handyman, but he was on a hunting trip. And Stu's colleague, who has been helping me with house and computer problems, was in London until next week. What else to do? I typed "How to Fix a Toilet Seat-*YouTube*" into Google, and a calm and sturdy man with a mustache appeared onscreen. He showed me how to lift the seat fasteners, remove the toilet seat and unscrew the bolts, one, two, three. "I can do this," I said aloud to the TV. "Just because I haven't, doesn't mean I can't." The man, so technologically soothing, put the new toilet seat in place, screwed in the new bolts and snapped the fasteners. Done.

I headed to the building supply store with my two toilet seats (to get the same ones), and a curly-haired salesman, my son's age, reaffirmed my conquering abilities. I believed him because last month, thanks to a *YouTube* video, I put a queen-sized duvet cover back on our bed. When Stu was alive, it was easy to stuff the freshly washed comforter into its cover and spread it across the bed. Stu would take one corner, I'd take the other, and we'd shake until every lump fell into place. But on my own, after thirty minutes of sweat and swearing, the comforter and duvet cover lay on the floor, a tangled mess. That is, until the *YouTube* showed me four simple folds. "It only takes one minute," assured the young woman from *Women's Day,* the video sponsor. Though I needed ten minutes to tuck the comforter into its rightful place, I felt triumphant.

Why not again? I said, and walked into the upstairs bathroom with toilet seat under arm and screwdriver in hand. The new bolts lay in wait outside the bathroom door. The toilet seat fit perfectly, and I felt Stu looking down, proud that I was managing on my own. He had worried that last year, giving me his passwords, making a list of bank accounts; he even tried teaching me Excel. But nothing about removing the toilet seat fasteners before me. I pushed and pulled; they didn't budge. And because they were plastic, I thought they might snap as had happened to Stu. He had extras; I did not.

"This was not like *YouTube!*" I said to myself, crestfallen, and lay down on the duvet cover, sideways, connecting what was his side to mine. It was dark when I woke up debating whether I should try again as I headed for the little half-bathroom, its one seat still intact.

How the Light Gets In

Of all the paths you take in life,
make sure a few of them are dirt.
—A POSTER QUOTING JOHN MUIR

We are at my kitchen table, sipping afternoon tea in the late October light. "How about Sicily in May?" I say, handing my sister-in-law a ten-day itinerary from my stash of travel brochures. She is keeping me company after I've had a premelanoma removed from my face. I wasn't going to do it, didn't want a new, ugly scar right after Stu died, and told everyone: "I'll take my chances. It is only 'pre'!" But I started hearing Stu in bed and in the shower: "Are you crazy? Do it!" So here I am with gauze taped to half my face, and Big Julie sleeping over so I won't be alone. I say Big Julie because our daughter is Little Julie, ever since Stu's brother Howie brought his girlfriend to our home for lunch almost fifty years ago.

"The trip looks great, but my newsletter is due then." Julie is communications editor for her school district and supercommitted to work after Howie died; it was last May, three months before Stu. So we are both feeling our way as "widows," a label I keep resisting, which is probably why I brought out the travel brochures.

"What about June, hiking in Croatia?" I hand her a Backroads catalog with a page dog-eared on the Dalmatian Islands. "I've hiked with them before."

"I'm free then," Julie says, "and I like hiking." We look at the blue shades of the Adriatic Sea and the tiny red roofs tucked into green hills below chalky cliffs. We see the hikers, young and old, along the high trail—and suddenly it's *Why not?* even as it feels like heresy, not what grieving widows are supposed to do. My mother cried and cried after my dad died, landing her in the hospital twice that first year. I love Stu, and Julie loves Howie; we feel our grief everywhere, lying in wait. Yet this trip feels right. "The men would approve," I say, pulling down the white kitchen shades over the black squares of window; the days are getter shorter.

Out comes Scrabble, a game Julie and I play whatever happens, online mostly; tonight we arrange the real tiles before us, feeling like adventurers. Maybe we'll stop in Rome, we say, before meeting the group in Dubrovnik. Julie has a friend who knows a small, friendly hotel off the Piazza Barbarini. It all seems doable—and safely eight months away. There's nothing to commit to, except the future.

It is really four of us, walking the streets of Rome with its ancient columns, ruins, and statues, awakening Rome's past and ours. Near the Spanish Steps, the marble breasts of Venus make me think of Stu at the swimming pool in Madrid, and as we walk, a story comes:

Did I ever tell you what happened to us in Spain? It was superhot, and there was a pool on the hotel roof, according to the concierge. So we climbed the stairs, walked down the hall, and through a small door, Stu first. Suddenly his face is two feet from a row of glistening bare breasts. Five huge German women were sunbathing and eating sausage sandwiches, full of delight. He was in shock; he didn't know where to look, not that they cared. They

probably never heard of Twiggy and Vogue's love of anorexic beauty. . . .
It was a really small pool, the size of a living room. We had to sidestep to
the water, trying not to laugh out loud at those breasts and bellies, so out
there. We giggled all day.

Julie and I talk, laugh and wander the backstreets aimlessly—except
when we must step off a curb. Two near-death experiences—one with
a motorcycle, one with a red Fiat—make us pay attention when the
crowd starts to cross as if by magic or desperation. No reassuring
traffic lights with blinking red or green hands tell us to stop or go.
Not around here.

At a corner hotel with geranium-filled window boxes, Julie says,
"I think we stayed here on our honeymoon." With a broad grin, she
remembers how Howie couldn't get over the gold faucets or the giant
gnocchi in the restaurant up the street. Her hair is short and silver
gray now, but I see the young woman with straight black hair down
to her waist that first day. Little Julie had one wish: to keep brushing
her hair all afternoon, and Big Julie let her, captivating us all.

A man whistles admiringly. "Not at us!" we agree, but then he tips
his hat, we wave, and Julie remembers:

Did I ever tell you how Howie caused an accident here? He wanted to take
my picture in front of the Coliseum, so he stopped the car. I got out, stood
there posing, and before he could snap, two passing cars hit each other.
Howie said, "Jump in!" And we made our getaway. He said the guys were
looking at me. I was mistaken for a Roman prostitute.

I love that good memories are tucked into statues and sexy whistles.
Yet remain wary of places we've been with our men, afraid of "the
vortex effect," as Joan Didion calls it, when something trivial "can suck
you into the darkness of an irretrievable yesterday." New restaurants,
new museums, and new landmarks are safer. We do go to the Sistine
Chapel, where Stu and I visited before it was restored. It was 1968,

our first trip without the kids, and we felt like newlyweds, albeit guilty ones who kept calling home from a phone booth in the hotel lobby.

Julie and I signed for an early morning Vatican tour before the crowds came. In the Sistine Chapel, we easily see God's and Adam's hands almost touching above us, the world almost in control. And straight-ahead, unobstructed, is the wall of "The Last Judgment," its grime and soot replaced by a bold clarity of color in motion. Naked bodies, mostly men, entangle each other in vibrant blues, greens, and yellow: one side going to Hell; the other, to Heaven. I half-hear Stu saying, "They all seem to be doing the same thing!" and I miss him, his quiet irony.

"Stu would have loved seeing the Chapel restored," I say, feeling wistful, as we walk in full sun along the Tiber from the Vatican to Tiberina, a tiny island in its middle. We've done four miles, we estimate, which is good for getting into shape for Croatia. "Howie would have loved the fig leaf story," says Julie. After Michelangelo died, the Church painted fig leaves on every genital, our tour guide said. Most were removed during restoration. "All that energy unsheathed!" We giggle, see a gelato stand and decide to stop, our new daily ritual. I order hazelnut and make my usual comment about Stu loving pistachio. "Howie too!" Julie says, before ordering chocolate chip. We continue on.

I didn't bring a camera, feeling no need. Two dozen boxes of travel slides sit in our attic; this trip is about the moment. Still, I borrow Julie's camera to take pictures of the Christian cross on top of the Egyptian obelisk and the saints on top of Vatican columns, where Roman gods once stood. Stu loved odd juxtapositions and incongruities. These photos are for him.

Julie and I do one thing we never could have done with our husbands: we stop at every shoe store we see. We enjoy imagining their dismay: *What again?* and linger as we try on a sandal here, a pump there, as if waiting for *C'mon* or *Hurry up!* We never buy a thing! These forays are total acts of defiance and revenge. Like my throwing out Stu's old, oversized orange couch that he refused to discard, no matter what I said. He should have stuck around.

Standing on the *Piazza del Popolo*, the People's Square, we open our guidebook and discover the Caravaggio Trail. It's the route that travelers, worldwide, follow to see all of Caravaggio's paintings from Milan to Rome to Malta, to Palermo, to Messina; he was always fleeing. Twenty-one of his paintings are in Rome, and two major works, it turns out, are in the church in front of us: the Santa Maria de Popolo. Moments later, we are inside a dark chapel, looking at how heaven and earth can be fused by a thin strand of natural light from a high window. The pale beam touches Saul in "Conversion on the Way to Damascus," lying in darkness on the ground before he becomes Paul. A sturdy workhorse and his groom bear witness to this conversion, so intensely real and yet surreal. Caravaggio, the guidebook says, knew this painting would hang on this spot, illuminating Saul's transformation. Which, although I don't realize it until I write down this story, is why we came: to undergo transformation, to find new selves.

On the other wall, there is a small box that, with coins, lights up "The Crucifixion of St. Peter." A giant cross, upside down, looms above us with an upside-down Peter, defiant and angry, nailed to it. I look at the nails, the dirty feet, and embrace his earthliness. You can be Jewish (me) or a lapsed Catholic (Julie) and relate to this burly Peter, who probably came from a nearby bar, where Caravaggio, the sixteenth-century bad boy, liked hanging out. Will the rope holding Peter be strong enough? Will it break, so everything comes crashing down as darkness swallows the scene? The lights go off, we are out of coins, so who can know anything?

But we are hooked—and follow the Caravaggio Trail to six more paintings, almost all of church tales that Caravaggio transforms into his own. It's what I love best, how he turns what's accepted into surprise: Madonna as a barefoot peasant or prostitute; her kneeling supplicants with dirty feet; a shoeless Jesus; an old horse's hind legs morphing into a man's legs; an innocent-looking girl stealing a man's ring. And everywhere, soiled hands touching the spiritual as light and dark clash and kiss the world of spirit entering ours.

At the airport, going to Dubrovnik, we study everyone with a backpack who might be on our trip, especially the young, the bearded, and those with half-laced boots. Not the gray-haired gentleman in a blue sports jacket with an American flag lapel pin on the bus (I'm standing, he's sitting, and he offers me his seat). Or the diminutive aging blonde that sits beside him in a pink Chanel suit. Hedge-fund types, too old for a hiking week. Yet there they are in the lobby of the Dubrovnik Hilton that afternoon, among the fifteen gathered for a group briefing with Katrina and Pamush, our Slovenian guides.

Seeing the old couple makes me relax. *We* won't be the laggers. Even better is when the twenty-something, Irish American girl asks, "How long are the daily hikes?" And then the six-foot Texan with a ten-gallon hat, no older than sixty, follows with, "What's the maximum elevation gain? How steep will trails be?"

Four to six hiking hours a day. Not more than 900-foot rises. We can handle that! Katrina talks about always bringing raingear, snacks, sunblock, hats, plenty of water, and I nod. We are prepared (I've even brought a whistle!)—until she mentions snakes. "A very big brown, not to worry. It is not poisonous." She laughs, with young and pretty charm. "But the little silver one with brown on back, bad. Fatal." This was not in the brochure. I hate snakes. *Who signed us on this trip?* I hear Stu and Howie chuckling: "You're here. Get over it!" as Katrina hands us walking sticks, "Very good for rocky trails and the snakes!" I take mine with enthusiasm. This is not an old, decrepit person's stick; this is a snake-killing stick.

The Hilton Imperial, 120 years old, is the first hotel in Dubrovnik built with electric lights. Outside, its façade retains Old World charm; inside, it looks like every Hilton I've stayed in, modern and anonymously efficient. It's why I'm drawn to old boutique hotels, like our little one in Rome, preserving history in seventeenth-century sideboards and hand-sewn needlepoints that line the breakfast room every morning.

The city gate into Dubrovnik is a three-minute walk from the hotel. Unlike Rome, which sprawls on seven hills, with sections of original wall here and there, Dubrovnik looks like a giant fairy-tale castle, full of turrets, spires, tiled roofs, and ramparts on a two-kilometer wall that encircles the city, population 42,000. It has kept out pirates and would-be invaders like the Venetians and Ottomans since the thirteenth century.

We walk through the Pile gate onto a wide, car-free street paved in marble tiles and full of artisans, charming restaurants, and shops, all very hip. We watch a bride, flat-nosed and hefty, looking radiant for a photo op, her veil blowing in the breeze as she poses with her slim, black-suited groom. Many brides come to this city for its romance, says Katrina. "Very popular for a proposal on Valentine's Day." Julie and I bumped into her on our way to the Maritime Museum, but she convinced us to go with her to a wine bar overlooking the sea. As waves crash against the wall below us, she tells us how progressive this city has been. It was the first port, aside from Venice, to abolish slave trading (1416). It set up an almshouse and orphanage, had the first quarantine hospital (1301), and its first pharmacy, opened in 1317, is still operating today. She knows this history.

Dubrovnik, in 1979, became a UNESCO World Heritage Site, committed to preserving its beauty and its history. A good thing, too, because UNESCO funds repaired many buildings that were damaged during the 1990s war after Yugoslavia splintered into Croatia, Bosnia, and Slovenia. Despite the city's neutrality (and the wall), it was not spared from attack, and Katrina points out the bullet holes in the thick stone. Quite a few! They are marks of survival that I missed before.

When I told New Jersey friends I was going on this trip, they said, "Why Croatia?" The initial truth was that it fit our schedule; the truth I told everyone was great hiking and beautiful vistas. Now I have another truth: to walk in a fairy-tale land by the sea, scarred by bullet holes that, like the scars almost healed on my face, are only a small piece of the story.

We are given a hiking sheet to follow.

> 0.0 Facing the water turn LEFT and continue walking through the parking lot, keeping water on your right
>
> 0.1 Continue STRAIGHT through the parking lot when road enters from the left.

The decimals make me uneasy. I'm the English major; decimals were Stu's territory. He'd be the one to read this sheet, getting us from A to Z. It was only without a map that we ran into trouble.

> *Did I ever tell you, Julie, when we ended up ten miles from the car in a thunderstorm? We were hiking Sunfish Pond with the kids; they were six and eight, and lightning was coming straight down. And that time in the Vosges Mountains in Alsace? We'd still be walking if I hadn't finally balked that it couldn't be this way. Stu was so sure, we would have ended god knows where. Men.*

Julie says that Howie would never hike. "Fishing, yes, hiking no." I say I love the satisfaction of taking one step, then the other. "It's getting lost I hate. Maybe because at four, I wandered away to Continental Avenue, crossed 108th Street and was found at the white bank."

We chat easily, knowing each other's landmarks and cast of characters without explanation. And then the road goes straight up, as in

45 degrees up, and everyone disappears except for the hedge-fund couple. Ten minutes into Day 1, and we four are gasping; this isn't even a mountain trail. We're still in a little village of stone houses and leaning cypress trees, our walking sticks useless on cement.

Turn RIGHT at three-way intersection uphill and immediately veer RIGHT uphill towards the church.

I would have missed it, but the hedge-fund man, who is really a retired Army colonel named Jeb, finds the turn. We decide to stick with Jeb, whatever his pace. The woman with him is "Not his wife!" she assures me. "I've had two husbands, that's plenty!" She adjusts her Tilly hat (which matches his). "Call me Boo. I'm from Malibu," she says, stretching out the boooo. There is a hint of Gloria Swanson in *Sunset Boulevard*—but Boo is a chatterer. Nails, hair, Rodeo Drive. I move ahead, leaving Julie, much too polite to stop listening, and wait around the bend. With the sea far below, the jagged hills above, I feel like the hiker in the brochure from my kitchen table. The glorious sky has not one cloud as we follow the single dirt trail that keeps winding around the mountainside.

Katrina or Pamush show up, we discover, whenever our sheet says EASY TURN TO MISS. This is a comfort, but we still stick with Jeb or stay in the middle of the group. The family of four always sprints ahead, as do the mother and daughter team, arriving an hour before us. By Day 3, we've mastered the sheet of instructions, and I have stopped clacking my pole to warn snakes, forgetting they are real until I spot the fatal, little silver one crushed by a tire on the road. Walking through the vineyards to the farmhouse where we are to eat lunch, someone sees the brown snake curled near the vines. It is big, at least eight feet and fat, but by then, I've become more curious than afraid. A pleasant fatalism has taken hold.

"What does it matter if I die?" I tell Julie on Day 4. "A weight has been lifted now that no one really depends on me."

"I'd miss you," she says. "So would your kids and grandkids."

I nod. But they're not little and with Stu gone, why not risk more, live in the moment and stop worrying—which takes me out of the moment. I trip, cut my finger on a rock, as if the Fates are saying, "Really?" I take out bacitracin and a Band-Aid, and Julie puts both on for me.

Pamush and I are walking through a sloping field full of lavender. He's a tall, curly haired young man with a degree in computer software, easygoing but looking serious now. "You have been married a long time, yes?"

"I have . . . was."

"May I ask advice?" I am wondering where this is going. He knows Stu died, so am I the wise widow who has figured marriage out?

"I love my girlfriend," says Pamush, taking long strides, "but she doesn't want children. I want three or four." The trail narrows, but we are still side-by-side. "I try to convince her—for three years—but she loves her job, a lab technician. So far she refuses."

I'd love to say *Go out with Katrina!* Since Day 1 our two guides have been so good together. She is full of energy; he, quietly steady. Not unlike how Stu and I are . . . were. I think:

> *How we filled in the missing pieces of each other. Stu as Mr. Calm, crushed the Tylenol into applesauce for our Baby Julie with 104 temperature after I had panicked. But the week before, after walking into her room and seeing blood on the crib sheets, he fainted. It was I, cool as could be, who applied pressure, stopped her nosebleed. So we knew: he did fever, I did blood—and it worked for fifty years.*

Aloud I say, "I'd ask myself whether I loved the person enough not to have children. What I wouldn't do is try to change her mind. Or keep waiting for her to decide. Both lead to bitterness."

A bit Dear Abby-ish, but you can't manufacture the missing pieces. That much I've learned. You shave a rough edge here and there, hoping for a smoother fit. That's it. I resist saying *Ask Katrina if she likes kids. There's no ring on her finger!* and we stop talking. The trail gets steeper with lots of rocks to make you lose your footing. We go single file.

For almost every lunch, we sit in rustic farmhouses at long tables filled with bowls of "secret family recipes." There are lamb stews, calamari, and amazing potato dishes (what have I been eating all these years?), homegrown zucchini, spinach, mushrooms, and tomatoes, all served hot and cold in a dozen ways. The only problem is three hours of hiking afterward, especially after two glasses (small) of homemade grappa in exotic flavors (walnut and rose are my favorites). At first I hear Stu warning. "Go easy. You know you fall asleep on this stuff!" but he fades with each sip. I do want to curl up under the largest tree, the one casting the biggest shadow—and then comes the family's Turkish coffee, Croatian style. Two cups of that, and I could climb Mount Everest, and from then on, it's grappa to start lunch, Turkish coffee to end it.

In these Dalmatian Islands, weather matters. With the rain, the sapphire sea edged in turquoise disappears; so do fields in a dozen lush shades from olive to basil green. So do the yellow Spanish broom and purple lavender everywhere, and the white chalk hills looking down like benign judges.

Luckily, it rains only twice. One morning, walking on a high ridge, a thunderstorm comes up quickly on our right. Pitch black clouds and a flash of lightning replace where the sea should be, while on the left, the blue sky stays blue. We are right under the storm's boundary and keep walking, feeling only a few raindrops. Yet the next day with the sun out, it pours suddenly, soaking us through. I think of Caravaggio, his chiaroscuro, light and dark, side by side, and how his art on the church walls is suddenly here. You can't predict when two worlds will bump each other, but I am dry fifteen minutes later, glad I invested in fast-drying clothes before this trip.

Not counting Katrina, the group has seven single women. There's Boo, close to eighty, and happily living with Jeb on her terms. There are the two young Irish girls who came to the United States as teenage au pairs and now run a small business. I like their laugh and the bounce in their walk, not at all like the tall, desperate Jill, midfifties, who keeps "joking" that she's "ready to snare a man." I make a mental note: Don't ever be like her. Or like the surly woman, late-thirties, traveling with her mother. I invent my story about her: that she's newly divorced, and her mom, a widow or divorced, is here to make her feel better. But one night at dinner, I'm proven wrong. Her problem isn't a man; she says it's the hikes. "I've climbed all forty-eight peaks in New Hampshire and was expecting more challenge." She smiles, for the first time, and I smile back—without one bit of regret about the trip's terrain. It's been just fine! In fact, Julie and I are thinking about another Backroads trip to somewhere *if* it's listed as 2–3 out of 5—easy to moderate—and we bring walking sticks. Which we have renamed: hiking poles.

Maybe on the last day, I am too confident. After all, we are confirmed middle-of-the-packers, never the last back to the bus or hotel. Maybe I have too much grappa at lunch, or the steep decline never seems to level off. But I keep slipping on stones even with my poles. I stop to adjust my inner heel lift, a gift from the Texan after my anklebone kept rubbing on the top of my right shoe. "Here, this will raise your foot a quarter of an inch," he said. Such a nice man, even if what he calls his "bear knife" is always on his belt.

He is nowhere in sight, nor is Julie or anyone else. She has walked ahead with Jeb talking about World War II (Boo quit after lunch. It was too hot, too steep, she said.). We are feeling more independent, especially today when getting lost isn't an issue. There is only one trail to follow: down to a beach, turn right and follow the shore trail to the hotel. Simple enough that Katrina and Pamush have also disappeared, not needed for intersections.

I conjure up Stu's favorite line: "You've got to play the hand that's dealt!" but my legs are not cooperating. They are beginning to cramp. I stop to take some water and remember my whistle is somewhere in my daypack. If I blow that, I'll be the helpless widow. Idiotic. I decide I'll keep moving, even as my legs start shaking as the ground keeps skidding out from me. What is the worst that can happen? *Oh, she died while hiking down a mountain in Croatia. Much better than ending while being turned over four times a day because of bedsores!!*

I feel a stab in my right knee from an old ski accident, and my sciatica has started to throb. Stu used to kid: "If you die first, I will put an ad in the paper: Woman Wanted Under Warranty." Well, his ran out; now mine, but I keep moving.

Suddenly I hear waves hitting the rocks. I can't look up for long, because now I'm on huge boulders with crevices big enough to disappear in. My legs refuse another step, and I freeze, as I did at Split Rock Gorge at age twelve, watching the water swirl over rocks twenty feet below. I had jumped so easily for four years, the bravest little camper, until the day I saw the consequence of a misstep—and backed away. I was twelve and never jumped again, avoiding the edges of everything that now surrounds me. I consider the whistle again. *I'm too old for this*—the first time I've ever believed it—and drop to my knees, too tired to think of where to step. I crawl across a smaller crevice—*I'm too old for this.*

And then I hear the laughter, loud and raucous, as if an audience is watching me, the old lady fool. I quickly stand, embarrassed, and see them: five sun worshippers in varying shades of bronze, buck naked and facing the sea. The men lie prostrate, like Neptune gods arisen from the sea, three muscled old men unsheathed on flat boulders. Two women, in silhouette, stand beside them, and I see nipples, bellies, and butts, neither young nor smooth. All five, close to my age, seem to revel in uninhibited bulges, wrinkles, and good cheer. And I am back in Spain with those bare-bosomed German women, and Stu not knowing where to look. Suddenly they see me, wave, and I wave back, giggling. To hell with my stretch marks and scars, I should join them.

Gone are my sharp rocks of consequence. The treacherous crevices are now just large cracks my legs span a dozen times without help, advice, or warning. I reach the soft pine needles, take the half-mile of shore trail still ahead, and the only sound I hear is my own laughter, urging me on.

Acknowledgments

I'm grateful to the many generous readers who helped to shape this book. A special thanks to Lynn Powell, Alice Ostriker, Tom Larson, Nancy Sommers, Julie Mazer, Julie Schwartz, and Ann Horowitz, who read the whole manuscript—and more than once! And to Richard Hoffman, Ladette Randolph, Edith Milton, Lois Harrod, Juditha Dowd, Dusty Smith, and Mindy Lewis, with whom I've regularly exchanged drafts over coffee, wine, and email. And to my astute and faithful friends like Gail Ullman, Rob Socolow, Penny Dugan, Hanan Ronel, Scotia Macrae, Susan Hockaday, and Sondra Perl, who always seem to say, "Sure, let me read it!" And to Vermont Studio and The Phillips Club for offering the setting needed to write. And to the wonderful team at University of Nebraska Press for their ongoing support, competence, and good cheer.

Source Acknowledgments

"Anthem" words and music by Leonard Cohen. Copyright © 1992 Sony/ATV Music Publishing LLC and Stranger Music Inc. All rights administered by Sony/ATV Music Publishing LLC, 424 Church Street, Suite 1200, Nashville TN, 37219. International copyright secured. All rights reserved. Reprinted by permission of Hal Leonard LLC.

"My Father Always Said" originally appeared in *Fourth Genre* 1 (Spring 1999). Copyright 1999 by Michigan State University.

"The Coronation of Bobby" originally appeared in *Creative Nonfiction* 5 (Spring 2015).

"Love in a Handbag" originally appeared in *Superstition Review* in 2008.

"When to Forget" originally appeared as "Forget" in *One Word—Contemporary Writers on the Words They Love or Loathe*, edited by Molly McQuade (Louisville: Sarabande, 2010).

"It's Just like Benheim" originally appeared in *When I Stepped on My Brother's Head and Other Stories Your English Teacher Never Told You*, edited by Charles Schuster and Sondra Perl (Portsmouth: Boynton/Cook Heinemann, 2010).

"First Thanksgiving, 1962" originally appeared as "There but for the Grace" in *Book of Worst Meals*, edited by Walter Cummins and Thomas E. Kennedy (Floral Park and Copenhagen: Serving House Books, 2010). Copyright 2009 Mimi Schwartz.

"What's a Rally to Do?" originally appeared in *Tikkun* 18, no. 3 (Spring 2003).

"In the Land of Double Narrative" originally appeared in *Tikkun*'s online magazine in May 2011, www.tikkun.org.

"Story on a Winter Beach" originally appeared as "Sharing Stories" in *New Jersey Monthly* (June 2002).

"Writing with Carly" originally appeared in *New Plains Review* (Fall 2008).

"My Z Man" originally appeared as "Your Z Man" in *You: An Anthology of Essays Dedicated to the Second Person*, edited by Kim Dana Kupperman, Heather Simons, and James Chesbro (Washington DC: Welcome Table Press, 2013).

"Who Will I Be in Your Story?" originally appeared as "Who Will Tell My Story?" in *TriQuarterly Online*, a publication of Northwestern University (Spring 2012).

"Echo across the Road" originally appeared as "When History Gets Personal" in *Agni* (Spring 2010).

"Ad In, Ad Out" originally appeared in the Summer/Fall Nonfiction Awards issue of *Solstice Magazine* (2014).

"On Stage and Off" originally appeared in *Prairie Schooner* 90, no. 3 (Fall 2016) and is reprinted by permission of the University of Nebraska Press. Copyright 2016 by the University of Nebraska Press.

"Lessons for a Last Day" originally appeared in *Pangyrus Online* (Spring 2017) and in the print edition in Winter 2017.

"A Vine of Roses" originally appeared in a special memoir issue of *Post Road* (2016).

"Fix-it Fantasy" originally appeared in *Persimmon Tree* (Winter 2017).

CPSIA information can be obtained
at www.ICGtesting.com
Printed in the USA
LVOW03s1102240118
563626LV00001B/1/P